MW01613248

HOW SNEAKERS SAVED MY LIFE

My Entrepreneurial Journey

An Autobiography By: TRENT

How Sneakers Saved My Life
My Entrepreneurial Journey

ISBN 978-1-7775245-0-0

First Edition

Published by:
Exclucity

Printed in Canada by Sure Print & Design

To My Mother –

With you I know there is at least one person who is always and forever, unconditionally, in my corner.

Contents

Foreword

Trent never ceases to amaze me. This book is poignant, personal, and meaningful. I didn't expect such honesty, drama, and humour all together, but then that is Trent.

I met Trent on my first trip to Montreal and my second day in my new role as one of the country's sales managers with Nike Canada. It started as a tough trip and Exclucity would bear the brunt of some critical eyes. It was tough because within three hours of arriving in Montreal with the corporate evaluation team, which included the most influential Sportswear sales directors at Nike, our computer bags, computers, and marketplace notes were stolen from our car. None of us was happy but the business must go on, even when you have a salty attitude.

It caught us off-guard as to how underdeveloped the Montreal sneaker landscape was at the time. There was a good boutique here and there but not really what we needed to impact the market. After a long day, we finally reached Exclucity. From the outside, it was not much, but we noted he had a consumer and trend source in the local secondary school right across the street. We weren't impressed with the store but were captivated by Trent, his energy, and what he was trying to do. When we walked out, we finally smiled that day. We knew we wanted to be with him; he could be the future of the marketplace. Trent proved us right.

I'm so happy for his growth and success. This book revealed a side of Trent I hadn't known but puts it all into perspective for me now, how he grew up and the hustle not to just make money but to be successful. Trent's knowledge through trial and error conveyed in his book represents creativity, consumer understanding, mad people skills, excellent business intuition, and tenacity at the highest level. I'm glad we made that first visit. I'm proud to have been a part of his business growth initially; more importantly, I'm pleased to be able to call him a friend today.

Good luck, Trent. I can't wait for the next editions.

Will Shelby
Former Nike Director

Foreword

I am a long-time entrepreneur at heart running my own record label and managing my brother, helping him get three Juno Award nominations and pushing him to reach his full potential. These are the kinds of things I've always excelled at.

When my music journey ended, I started at NIKE as an account manager and after a few years I got the opportunity to move to Montreal as a sales rep. That move to Montreal was the opportunity that I needed so that I could show the executives at Nike what I could do in a market which I felt had a lot of untapped potential, using the tools I learned from running my label and managing my brother. What I looked for and needed to find in an "Artist" was someone that had the passion, work ethic, vision and desire to do whatever it takes to move things to the next level. Now, I just needed to find someone like that in the sneaker world!

Here is where the story begins.

I wanted to make a name for myself at Nike but I needed an account, an owner that wanted the same thing. When I met Trent all the qualities I was looking for were present. He had a strong work ethic and was focused on nothing else but growing his company to be #1 in Canada. When the journey began it was never about the money or the props for Trent; he always wanted to personally fly under the radar. It was about reaching unimaginable levels of growth for his brand and that is precisely what transpired in the four years we worked together.

Exclucity disrupted the marketplace and made so much noise that top executives from NIKE would hear of this brick-and-mortar shop and made it a point to visit anytime they set foot in Canada. Trent even became a major thorn in the side of a major national corporate company, lol. The momentum he created was something no one had ever come across and will probably never see again. I'm glad to have been a part of it.

Nick Nestor
Former Nike Territory Sales Rep

Foreword

Man, where do I start? I guess with Long Tees and Du-Rags.

When Exclucity (formerly known as Hip Hop Exclusive) first opened, it was 2006 and I was 14 years old. I don't know about y'all but my mom was buying my clothes so we need to fast forward a year or two later when I started shopping for myself.

Now by this time I'm attending a high school that's very multicultural. The school was heavily populated by Black kids with hip-hop culture having a significant influence on the way we spoke and dressed. To put it bluntly, it was a hip-hop school. Even the white kids were into hip-hop. I remember all of us being so young and impressionable, following everything we see on TV or heard in music.

I can recall rushing back home after school just to catch music videos on BET Freestyle Fridays. Those were my favourite times! R.I.P to that show, that channel was so iconic back in that era, especially for black music.

So now I'm 16,17, trying to swag out and look like my favourite celebrities but I lived in the suburbs which is pretty far from the city (Downtown Montreal). Having Exclucity open up in the West Island of Montreal was way more accessible for me, and those who didn't drive.

Back in those days, long tees and du-rags were huge. It's funny when I think back to all the arguments my friends would have on who has the most and every week that number would increase. When I tell you everyone had one I mean EVERYONE.

Even back before the official opening of the store, I'm talking about when Trent was selling out the trunk his car days, my school was flooded with long tees and I know my school wasn't the only one.

To help paint a better picture of the impact Exclucity made, my principal literally had to make an amendment to our school uniform regulations to allow us to start rocking the white long tees and Dickies' pants that everyone copped from Exclucity.

Exclucity came through with the biggest variety I've ever seen. They had long tees in all sorts of colours. You would see kids rocking their favourite colour long tee underneath their uniform and everyone knew where that long tee came from -- Exclucity. Super baggy was in those times so even if I was a medium I'm ordering my stuff in 2XL. What better way to pair an oversized tee with some baggy pants so that you can't see my underwear, it was a beautiful thing!

There were a few other stores around where I could get one or two things, but not one specific store where I could get a whole outfit. That was the amazing thing about Exclucity, they always had everything you needed. They had, earrings, chains, grills, they even had the belt with the freaking digital words that you can type in on the belt buckle that you see on TV, if you know you know! There were jeans, shoes, and more. Honestly, anything hip-hop you can think of, Exclucity had it. Even the hard to find items that you probably only find in the States, Trent had it. Exclusive wasn't in the name for no reason.

I know back in those days to get exclusive stuff a lot of parents would take their kids to New York, however, for kids like me we weren't that fortunate. To have a store like Exclucity in my own area, so close to my house, it was amazing.

This was the age before social media so you would see Exclucity posters, stickers, and flyers as the store started gaining some traction and it quickly became a lot of people's go-to spot for the flyest gear!

Re'shaun D.
A "Day One" Exclucity loyalist

Foreword

If someone had told me my brother, Trent, would have a passion for reading books, much less writing them, I would have thought they were crazy! To be honest, when I really think about it and especially knowing the person Trent is, I am not really surprised. Trent has always been a passionate and knowledgeable person wanting to teach, coach and impart wisdom onto others… and that is exactly what he has done with this book.

LOL… I wish I could write this part without him seeing, but… Trent is my little brother (and will always be my LITTLE brother even when he becomes a renowned Pulitzer Prize-winning author) and I am truly and incredibly proud of him and all that he has accomplished. As you will read in this book, he has faced many challenges in his life (albeit some of them self-inflicted), but he has always been able to learn and better himself with each experience. I consider myself a strong person, but Trent has faced challenges and taken risks that I would never even consider. Words cannot describe how much I admire him for that.

I am truly proud of Trent, but most importantly I am very proud to be his sister and even prouder that he is my best friend.

Enjoy the book.

Preface

Everyone dreams, but not all of us fight.

Thirteen years ago, I started writing a self-help book because I've always been very frustrated, and still am today, when I see people not living or fighting to live their truth. It pisses me off to no extent. Because of said anger I set out to write a self-help book in hopes that people would read it, feel inspired, and then go out and start living their purpose.

My self-help book never got completed because in the back of my head I knew it SUCKED! Years later, not wanting to give up, I tried turning the book into YouTube vlogs, then an Instagram Meme page, and more recently, an Instagram page where I tried to mix my personal and business life while trying to be motivational, BUT none of it worked. It was all a complete disaster.

Then COVID-19 hit.

March 16, 2020 was my first day of quarantine after landing back in Montreal from Barbados. After a few months of quarantining I realized that I was probably going to be in my house for the rest of the year, and I had a genius idea. I thought, quarantine would be the perfect time for me to finally finish my book. I told myself that it was because I was so busy for the past thirteen years why I couldn't finish it, forgetting that it wasn't time that was the problem, it was me. I wasn't good at giving people a step-by-step tutorial on fighting to live their truth.

Before remembering my shortcomings, I sat down to write the first chapter of my book and I started it off with my grandmother. But this time, for some odd reason, it felt like I was telling a story -- my story. I was writing from a personal perceptive and I wrote for days nonstop. Everything that I had been struggling to say for the past 13 years was finally pouring out of me, effortlessly.

I gave the first twenty pages to a friend to get some feedback and she immediately said, "OMG, YESSSSS. FINALLY. This is how you need to write your book. You have to be Trent and speak in your voice. I know you're really private, but you have a great story that people can learn from and will want to hear."

. . .

With everything I've ever done, I've always had something to hide behind. I was an international model, and yes, I was in front of the camera but I hid behind the clothes. I built Exclucity, a multi-million-dollar national brand, but I hid behind the logo. Not even my social media is really me. I take twenty pictures, scroll through them, find the best one, then post it.

I wanted this book to be different.

This book is the first time in my life that I'm not standing behind anything and just being me. I wanted it to be me, standing in front of you as me. If you hate me, I'm ok with that, and if you love me then I'm ok with that also, but at least I know you love me or hate me for **me**, and that is the most amazing feeling in life.

As I looked deeper into my life to write this book, I got really nervous when it came to certain moments from my past. There were things in my life, like being on welfare, that I never told a soul. And then there were things that only my immediate family knew about, like my father being physically abusive towards my mother, and other things like me being at such a low point in my life that I was living in an attic and showering at the YMCA. Writing about those things makes me feel super vulnerable, hence the reason I kept my life so private before this book, even with my closest friends.

It's hard to be open. I want you to think I'm strong and resilient; I don't want you to know that I am dyslexic. Nor do I want you to know about my not-so-perfect childhood, my insecurities, what makes me nervous, my fears, or the times in my life when my stomach dropped. I'm getting that feeling in my stomach right now. I hate it, but I'm learning those moments of vulnerably are when you're at your purest, the real you.

This writing process taught me that vulnerability makes you feel naked, but it also makes you feel free.

In this book, I write about things I've done in my past that I'm not proud of. I hesitated putting some of it in here, as I feared people would think I'm trying to glorify it, which is simply not the case. Telling you that I've been charged with carrying an illegal firearm doesn't make me feel cool; it scares the shit out of me. I've never told anyone that before. I fear that people will judge me, or that I may lose some of my business partnerships but I made the hard decision to speak about them regardless because these are my mistakes, my truths and my journey.

. . .

My self-help book turned into an autobiography because I had a hard time creating a step-by-step guide. I'll leave that to Tony Robbins, he's good at it. I don't know how to tell you how to be the best you, only you can do that. We are all different.

If I can help someone to not make the same mistakes I did, or push somebody to move past their own mistakes from telling my story, then the purpose of this book has been accomplished.

. . .

Success is right around the corner from defeat.

TRENT 1 | Growing Up in Pain

Growing Up in Pain

July 5,1924 is the date that my grandmother on my mother's side was born. I'm highlighting it because my grandmother is the only person in my family that they say I'm exactly alike. Some would argue I'm more like my dad but that's only in personality. If you dig deeper, at the core, I am Ethlyn Rosetta Harris.

My grandmother was an entrepreneur in Jamaica. She sewed dresses from her own patterns and with the leftover material she'd make underwear, skirts, pants and shirts for herself and her family. My family comes from a level of poverty that most of you do not know. My grandmother was born in Cocoa Walk in Manchester, Jamaica, a rural community which many called "the bush." The community had one post office and one grocery store and if residents needed anything else they had to travel to the closest city, Mandeville.

In the 1920s, in Cocoa Walk, there were no welfare cheques, government assistance programs or food banks. When you were poor, you were poor and on your own. There was no electricity, the bathroom was outside in the backyard, and the roof of your house could blow off whenever the weather was windy. There were many nights when my mother had to hold a kerosene lantern for my grandmother so she could finish her sewing for her clients. This was a normal way of life for them.

Stories, like these, drive me to wake up early every morning to make sure I hustle my ass off and never take anything for granted. I think today's generation takes for granted what our parents and grandparents had to do for us to be where we are today. As a result, I believe that it's our duty to take whatever opportunity they gave us and work just as hard so that their efforts were not in vain.

If your parents busted their ass to raise you in an apartment, it's your duty to bust your ass to buy a house in which you can bring up your kids. Let's keep it real; they didn't have the Internet, cars, smart phones, and Uber Eats. No matter how hard our life gets, it's nothing compared to what they had to go through.

Which brings me to my next story about my grandmother.

After realizing that sewing wasn't going to give her the life she wanted, my grandmother started growing tobacco, which was more profitable for her at the time. But that still wasn't enough and my grandmother grew tired of the never-ending struggles that plague Jamaica until today. All that my grandmother wanted was to make enough money so she could leave the island. That was her only mission in life; as a single mother, all she wanted was a better life for her two daughters and future grandkids. She wanted something different for us and knew that if she wanted generational change she'd have to get out of her comfort zone. My grandmother knew that she needed to take a leap of faith. One day she heard about an opportunity in Montreal, Canada that could possibly free her from those struggles.

. . .

In 1955, the Canadian Government launched the West Indian Domestic Scheme, "a targeted immigration program through which approximately 3,000 women from the Caribbean came to Canada to work as domestic servants." The program ran from 1955-1967. At the time, my grandmother had no idea that her rights -- civil and human – would be so violated by this poorly regulated program. She blindly trusted the Canadian government out of desperation and applied right away.

Before she did so, however, there was a problem. The interviews were being held 15-20km away from where she lived and she didn't have proper footwear for the long walk. Not letting something like that get in her way, my grandmother borrowed her neighbour's shoes – men's shoes that were four sizes bigger than her feet.

My grandmother made it to the interview but, unfortunately, her application was not accepted right away. Something happened with some lying women in the line and although my grandmother put up a fight, she lost her place and didn't make the final cut. Fortunately, the following year, the Canadian government returned to Jamaica for a second round and my grandmother was finally accepted.

Within days of the acceptance, my grandmother had to fly to Canada leaving behind her two daughters, mother, brother, sister and cousin. She vowed to not only send money back for them weekly but to one day bring them all to Canada so that they could eventually become Canadian citizens.

. . .

As soon as my grandmother landed in Canada, she was placed with a rich white family. I can only guess what must have been going through her mind; the culture shock alone must have been so difficult for her. Selfishly, the family she was placed with didn't take the time to think about any of this or the time that it would take for her to adjust. It was just straight to business like she wasn't even human. They never even considered her feelings.

When they got home from the airport, the family gave her a tour of the house she would be responsible to clean and maintain. They also introduced her to the three kids that she would be taking care of daily. She was shown her "bedroom," which was really a hallway closet. There was just a single mattress on the floor with no space for a bedside table or other furniture.

The family didn't let her eat the same food she prepared for them, nor was she allowed to sit at the same table as them. People of colour weren't allowed at their table.

Afraid to say anything to avoid being sent back to Jamaica, my grandmother kept quiet and she continued working.

I HATE that she had to go through that.

. . .

My grandmother's first year in Canada was brutal. Whenever she spoke about it, you could still hear the pain in her voice. You could tell that she was still very bitter and angry towards that family, especially the wife who was always nasty towards her. She wouldn't hesitate to call her all kinds of bad names; it was even funny at times.

The thing I admired most about my grandmother's story is the way she told it, she was neither ashamed nor felt belittled by it. She made you feel like it was nothing to her and that the woman had no effect on her at all. My grandmother knew she had to play the game, and she wasn't going to let this family break her down.

Break who down? Not Ethlyn Rosetta Harris. It was upwards and onwards because there was a mission at hand, her family.

Regardless of how difficult that first year was, my grandmother stayed with that family until her one-year probation was over. As soon as she passed her one-year anniversary, she went to the government office to file a complaint and demanded to be sent to another family.

The other domestic workers thought she was crazy for even saying a word but Ethlyn Harris wasn't about that bullshit, AT ALL! She knew that after her probation ended they couldn't just send her back to Jamaica. It was time for her to put her foot down and demand to be placed with a better family.

She eventually found a family that respected her human rights and provided her with a bedroom and adequate food. However, I am still mad that she couldn't make demands for her civil rights, but I know things were different then. We fight the fights we can, and plot out how to win the others in the future.

One of Ethlyn's favourite quotes was, "You have to kiss ass, before you can kick ass." Although she knew that she personally wouldn't be able to kick ass here in Canada, (the system wouldn't allow that), she knew that if she kissed ass long enough, I'd be able to kick ass for her.

. . .

My grandmother wasn't paid very much for her services but she saved what she could. She survived with the bare minimum while trying to take care of and feed six people back home in Jamaica. My grandmother's life is an example that the path to success is never easy. The journey is slow and gruelling but because of her I know dreams get closer each day as we struggle towards them.

Ethlyn Rosetta Harris died on May 2, 2016 at the age of 91.

. . .

My Mother

In 1961, my grandmother fulfilled the promise that she made before she left for Canada. She sponsored and paid for my mother, my aunt and her sister, and later her brother and cousin to come to Canada and live permanently. It was a huge undertaking but she got it done. They didn't have the luxury we have today of being allotted time to sit back, relax, and figure out what they wanted to do. Since they were all under my grandmother's care, they all had to get jobs quickly so they could eat and keep a roof over their heads.

. . .

Fast forward many years later when my mom had a family of her own and not much had changed. My mom was constantly struggling to make ends meet and keep a roof over her head. She worked in the maternity ward at the hospital taking care of newborns. As a nurse, her job consisted of changing bedpans and cleaning up after people, but she loved her role and took great pride in it. My mom barely made above minimum wage and worked overtime 2-3 times per week just to make ends meet. She could have made more money as a registered nurse but she could not afford the tuition and she didn't know how to speak French.

To make things worse, my mother worked the evening shift 3 p.m.-11 p.m. at the hospital because my parents couldn't afford a babysitter. My dad worked days and my mom worked nights. From childhood to young adulthood, I grew up with my mom not being at home with me after school or at night. I hated it but I knew she was doing it for her kids so I dealt with it.

My mother and grandmother had a plan for my sister and me before we were even born. They sacrificed themselves for us so we could have the opportunity to be great. They knew that they wouldn't be able to give us much money or privilege, but they knew if they gave us an opportunity, we'd handle the rest ourselves. That's why until today I don't believe in traditional luck. Yes, you can get lucky buying a lotto ticket and winning, but getting into the NBA isn't luck. That's preparation and opportunity coming together at once. I got that from Oprah and if you don't believe it, I suggest reading Malcolm Gladwell's *Outliers: The Story of Success* if you want a thesis on the subject.

. . .

As a kid, when I got home from school, there was never a day that dinner wasn't left out on the kitchen counter for us. Even though my mom wasn't home from 3 p.m.-11 p.m., it was like she was always there with us in spirit.

In elementary school, I remember waking up every morning and my clothes would be laid out for me on my bed. My mom would be in the kitchen waiting for me in her nightgown, sipping a cup of tea with my breakfast ready and my lunch packed. She'd do the same for my sister.

At breakfast, my mom always talked to me about my homework and how school was going, although all I wanted to talk about were the girls that I liked. We always had a close relationship like that; it was amazing. I could talk to my mom about almost anything and she'd be right there listening to me. It's a difficult balance for a parent to be friendly with their child and not lose that parental respect, but my mother aced that and walked the line perfectly.

. . .

With all the good that my mother brought to our family and as amazing as she is, unfortunately, my father never appreciated her and always took her for granted. As a result, they had a very toxic, physically and verbally abusive relationship.

Despite everything my father put my mother through, she always put my sister and me first and tried to shield us from everything that was going on between them. But there are certain things you can't hide in an abusive relationship, and as a result, as kids, we both saw things that no child should ever have to see their mother deal with.

As a little kid growing up not understanding what abuse was, I remember thinking my dad was a superhero. I followed him around everywhere but all that stopped when I saw him hit my mom for the first time. I think that's when the cape came off and he was no longer my hero. I started hating him.

My mother would never say anything bad about my father, regardless of what he did to her. She'd just suppress it all so that my sister and me could grow up with happy memories of our childhood.

I know now that had it not been for us, my mother would have divorced my father much earlier, but she made the sacrifice for us and waited until we were older to leave him. That's not the right thing to do but it's what she thought was best at the time.

It's not fair that my mother never got the chance to live the life that she deserved. She is worthy of way more than my father gave her.

I hate that my mother felt she had to stay in a physically abusive relationship with someone that cheated on her relentlessly, just for her kids' sake. I wished that my mom was born in today's world with women empowerment and had the tools to deal with her marriage in a better way.

I just wish.

. . .

My mom is by far the best mom ever; even my sister who is a mother of four thinks so, lol. She's just a good human being. Until today, I've never heard my mom say anything bad about anyone, and Lord forgive me if I criticize someone, she would let me know that I shouldn't say that.

When we were kids, my mom couldn't afford to buy my sister and me brand name clothes. All of our stuff came from Cohoes, a discount store. But regardless of how broke my mother was, we always got one BIG Christmas gift, and it would be whatever we asked for (in moderation, lol). That would tide us over until the next year.

Reminiscing on those times, I think they did me well because today I don't need to be dressed up or to wear a Louis Vuitton belt to feel confident. I know what I bring to the table, that's something my mother always taught me. She always said, "The clothes don't make the man, the man makes the clothes." I'll never forget that.

My mom was always focused on preparing me for the harsh world, and making sure I'd know how to navigate through it. It was her mission in life, still is.

Fun Fact:

My favourite memory from childhood was sneaking out of bed at midnight when my mom got home from work at night. She'd let me lie down with her on the couch watching the shows she taped because she was at work. She'd let me stay up as late as I wanted to and then she'd bring me to bed whenever she was going. My mom and I are still night owls until today. Recently, I called my mom at one o'clock in the morning for no reason at all, and she answered like it was three o'clock in the afternoon.

. . .

My Father

My father and I have a very complex relationship but I love my dad for who he is and everything that he's given me. I'm super blessed to have had my father in my life when I was growing up, and to still have him in it today.

My father grew up in Kingston, Jamaica, but he also spent part of his childhood in the countryside. He lived in a one-bedroom house with 11 family members, including his grandparents, his mom, his aunts and cousins. Like my mother's family, they were also very poor. He was the first of many grandkids.

My father's life started out with trauma and a lot of pain. But back in those days, parents had no idea the effects their actions had on their children's lives and future. My dad's mother was only 19 years old when she gave birth to him and his father was 40 years old, twenty-one years older than her. As a result, they rushed to get married but when my dad's mother's family found out the age difference between them, they freaked out and forced her to get the marriage annulled. She was forbidden to ever see my dad's father again.

To make matters worse, my dad's mother's family took him away from his father at birth and they gave him their last name as if my dad's father didn't exist.

Later in life, my dad would reconnect with his father, but needless to say my dad didn't have the typical upbringing that most little boys deserve. This is probably why we had issues while I was growing up, and why my parents would eventually get divorced. It's hard to be a dad when you don't have a point of reference, and equally so to be a husband.

Although there was trauma in his childhood, there was also a lot of positivity. His mother raised him in a very loving home with her parents, brother, and five sisters.

Growing up around mostly women, my father tried to assume the leadership role in the house. There wasn't much for a kid to do for money but everyone did what he or she could to pitch in, even youngsters.

As a kid, one of the things my dad and his friends did to make some pocket money was to swim around the docked cruise ships hoping that the tourists would throw them some change. The crew of the ships would show the mainly white passengers "the little Black boys diving for money." They would throw change into the water and watch the kids dive for it.

. . .

My dad's mother had the same ambition as my other grandmother, Ethlyn, and she did whatever she could do to get out of Jamaica, with dreams of a better life for herself and my dad.

She studied nursing in Jamaica and later moved to England where she gained a Bachelor's degree in Nursing at the Royal Free Hospital. Upon completion of her studies, she moved to Montreal, Canada to work as a nurse. A few years after being settled, my dad's mom would also fulfill her promise by sending for my dad and obtaining his citizenship in Canada.

I come from a lineage of strong Black women.

. . .

Like my mom, when my dad moved to Canada, he had to get a job so he could help pay the bills at home. He also followed in his mother's footsteps and went to school, but not for a trade, as his mother wanted him to get a degree. That was the deal.

Things were tough back then and my dad could only go to night school, but the messed-up part was that the only job he found was at night also. He left straight from school at eleven o'clock to go to work the midnight shift on a golf course picking worms throughout the night for fishermen.

My dad did a few odd jobs here and there as he went to university to pursue a degree. A few times he wanted to just drop out and work full-time but he remembered the deal he had made with his mom. Since she had a degree, he would have to pursue postsecondary studies as well, and she told him his kids would have to have at least two degrees, and so on. She was very focused on education, and wanted her family to thrive.

. . .

My Relationship with My Father

Because of my grandmother, my dad has always been a huge advocate for education.

My sister was on the honour roll every year and she achieved over 85% throughout every level of schooling. I, on the other hand, was always skipping classes, in detention, and would eventually get kicked out of high school to do home schooling. As a result of my shortcomings, my dad tried to discipline me, but chose to be an authoritarian instead of being authoritative.

Authoritative *parents teach and guide their children.* ***Authoritarian*** *parents, however, exert control through power and coercion. They have power, because they exert their will over their children.*

adjective: ***authoritarian***

favouring or enforcing strict obedience to authority, especially that of the government, at the expense of personal freedom.

My father, being both an authoritarian parent and an abusive husband, made our house a very toxic environment to live in. Things were really bad and there was a moment in my life when I just wanted to leave everything behind and get out.

My father was always frustrated with me, yelling at me and he'd always compare me to others and often ask me why I couldn't be more like them. I always felt less than and like I was such a major disappointment to him. I never felt good enough to live up to my father's expectation of what a son should be and that really hurt me.

In my early teens, I always wanted to get away from my father and would beg my mother to divorce him so we could go live on our own. There was always so much toxicity around my father and in our house, I wanted out. I didn't even want my sister to live with us; I just wanted it to be my mom and me.

One night, things got so bad that I couldn't take it anymore. I put my karate belt around my neck, tied the other end to the handle of my bedroom door and slowly leaned forward. I remember feeling dizzy and then I was on the floor.

I wanted it all to end.

. . .

The next day, I told my friend at school what I tried to do, and out of concern she told the principal, not realising that would only make matters worse for me at home.

I was called to the principal's office to see a social worker and after spending hours talking, the social worker told me they had to contact my parents and tell them what I had done. I begged and pleaded for them not to but my efforts were in vain.

It was downhill from there.

My mom, dad, sister and I had to do family counselling. They came to my house and my dad was not happy about that AT ALL. I was not only scared of what he would do to me after they left, but I was more concerned about my mom being hurt and being worried about me. I never wanted to scare her or to stress her out; she had enough to deal with regarding my father.

To this day, I remember my mother holding me and bawling her eyes out after the social worker left. She said, "Is it so bad here that you want to end your life, what did I do wrong?" I told her it wasn't that bad and that I was just being stupid. But I only told her that because I didn't want her to feel guilty. It was really that bad. I wanted to be away from my father so badly and at that age it was the only solution I could think of.

And how did my dad react to all this? Just as I feared he would, he got really pissed off at me. I can remember him saying, "I can't believe you'd bring these people into my house," as if that should be the concern.

My dad is forever playing the victim.

. . .

My father had very strict rules for me when I was a child. Education always came first and if I had 10 pages of a book to read for a school assignment, he'd try to make me read 20 pages to be ahead of the class. He wouldn't tolerate sleeping in, EVER. My sister and I had to be up early on the weekends to help around the yard or do something helpful inside the house. "Life isn't easy, you need to learn the value of hard work," he'd say.

I also had authoritarian guidelines to follow as well: NO sagging jeans. NO designs in my hair. I was not even allowed to grow out my hair. NO oversized clothes. NO slang talking. NO jewelry. NO NOTHNIG! I wasn't even allowed to wear my hat backwards. If I wanted to live under his roof, I had to follow all his rules. My dad and I got into a lot of physical fights as I got older over his rules.

Hating all those rules and because we had such a bad relationship, I finally moved out of my parents' house at 17 years old, but that didn't work out so well.

I quickly found out that the real world is not much easier than living under my dad's roof with all his rules.

Within the first year that I moved out, I started seeing all of the things that my dad was trying to warn me about when I was younger, like the importance of having an education and a well-paying job. Living on your own really wakes you up and shows you what life is really about; it was all starting to make sense to me.

I was realizing that my father just wanted the best for me, like my mother did, but he just didn't have the tools to deliver his message properly. At the time, I had no idea that my dad was looking out for me and trying to steer me in the right direction.

When I was 19 years old, two years after living on my own and making a mess of my life, I took my father out for a beer and told him that I was sorry for not listening to him when I was younger. Although I didn't agree with his methods, had I known then what I know now, I would have listened.

As overbearing as my father was, he also taught me a lot of good things, such as hard work, dedication and being relentless. I also learned the gift of the gab, to always be polite and charming, and that having a winning personality is key above all else. There is no way I'd be the entrepreneur I am today without my father.

Regardless of whatever stage I'm at with my father, it will never take away from the fact that he tried to be the best dad he could be with the tools he had, which were not very much. He didn't have a father growing up so he had no reference, I try to keep that in my mind as much as possible, but sometimes he makes it hard for me to do.

. . .

Me

Now that I've told you about my family, I guess the next logical step would be to tell you about me.

Here is a quick recap of my life.

These words are purposely not in order. Just think of each word as a puzzle piece, and by the end of this three-part book series I'll put all the pieces of the puzzle together.

Multi-Millionaire | Poor | Jamaica | Stealing | Jail | No food | Mice | Guns | Crack Cocaine | Police | Black | New York | Girls | Sex | More Sex | Weed | Drugs | China | Alcohol | Mansion | Cadillac | Jacuzzi | Rap | Toronto | Reggae | Abuse | $3.52 in the bank | Engaged | Montreal | Abortion | Range Rover | Failing (in school) | Dogs | Therapy | Filing for bankruptcy | Attempted Suicide | Family | Friend | Football | Over-Ambitious | Millionaire | Long Tees & Du-Rags | Liars | Honest | Mental Health | Dieting | Eating Disorder | Modelling | LaSalle | Ethlyn Rosetta Harris | Living in an attic | 2020 | Books | Marathon | Bipolar | Embarkation (special needs program in high school) | Athlete | COVID-19 | Hiring consultants | Drop-out | South Africa | Porn Star | Gunshot to the head | Drinking & Driving | Multiple car accidents | Winning addict | Gambling | Arson | Condoms | Lamborghini | Entrepreneur | Dyslexic | R&B | Losing $2 million | 2018 | Welfare | Toxic relationships.

EXCLUCITY 1 | Building A Startup

Building A Startup

The nuance of entrepreneurship has the ability to break the strongest of people. No matter how smart you are, or how much education you have, opening up a business and building a brand is one of the hardest things to do.

The startup process will be some of the most gruelling years of your business and there is no school in the world that can ever prepare you for it. You either have it in you or you don't. The ups and downs are relentless, exhausting and will consume every hour of your day.

Having said all that, if you have the stomach to deal with it, the drama is invigorating, and if successful, it will bring you higher than any drug ever could. Breaking through those taxing years and becoming profitable will make you feel like superman.

The first years of any business are when the foundation of your brand is built. Those are the years of sleepless nights when you feel like giving up, but you don't! Those are the years that you talk about the most in your book when you're writing your autobiography.

Before Exclucity became one of Canada's biggest sneaker boutiques, it was called Hip Hop Exclusive. Prior to that, it was AAA Styles, and before all of that, I sold Long Tees and Du-Rags from the trunk of my Honda Accord. To make it all happen, I lived in an attic, managed a rapper, modelled and made a tonne of sacrifices along the way. My highs where high but my lows were much lower, so low that I had to go on welfare just to get by.

Here's how I went from the selling of clothes from the trunk of my car to owning a multimillion-dollar national brand.

This is my startup journey.

Victor - Part 1

Montreal, June 2003

I used to volunteer at the YMCA as a basketball coordinator and one day a kid, Victor, came up to me and said, "Yo, you're the guy that sells used cars, right?" I replied, "Yes."

I had owned a small used car broker business but Victor didn't want to buy a car from me. He wanted to talk to me about business and to learn how he could become an entrepreneur. Most successful entrepreneurs have many failed businesses before they succeed. I've had a lot of failures so I was happy to offer some help.

At every basketball practice Victor would make it a point to either come in early or stay late to talk to me about business. He had questions such as: "How did you start? Do you need a business plan? How much money do I need?" He never stopped asking me questions, which was annoying but I admired his passion.

One day, Victor told me he had a proposal that he thought I'd be interested in and asked if I could sit down with him to talk about it. I asked him what it was about, and he said, "Selling T-Shirts." At that moment, I wanted to walk away but I let him continue. "I sell Long Tees & Du-Rags to my friends at school and I need a loan. If you would lend me $5,000 so I can buy in bulk, I'll pay you back with interest," he said. I looked at Victor as if he couldn't be serious. I really thought he was just joking and told him to get his butt back out on the court. I liked Victor a lot but he was just a16-year-old kid at the time. I wasn't going to give him $5,000 to buy T-Shirts to sell to his friends at school.

Victor bugged me week after week about lending him the money and I just kept saying no. He was so persistent that after a few weeks I finally got fed up and said, "Ok, let's sit down and talk about this seriously, and then if it's still a NO, we'll never talk about this again." He agreed.

To my surprise, when I met with Victor I quickly understood that he wasn't just selling regular T-shirts. These Long T-shirts were very popular and in heavy demand. What piqued my interest even more was that these Long Tees were only available in the USA and they were almost impossible to find in the Montreal area.

In business, if you're not manufacturing your own product, you should try to sell something that has controlled/limited distribution. If a product is only available in another country, that's even better. You'll have a competitive edge over the competition or even a monopoly (yes, like the board game).

Long Tees were the craze back in the day and every kid wanted them, especially Montreal kids that couldn't find them anywhere in the city at the time.

For those of you who don't know what Long Tees are, let me explain. Well actually, I can show you better than I can tell you. Just Google this video "Dem Franchize Boyz - White Tee."

Not only did Victor have a solid product, but he also had a lot of repeat business from the school kids in the area. Having all that meant that Victor's business had a system. Once you have a system, your next step is to grow that system with finances. Victor was right, his business was ready for some seed money.

Seed Money:

Seed funding is the first official equity funding stage. It typically represents the first official money that a business venture or enterprise raises. You can think of the "seed" funding as part of an analogy for planting a tree.

Seed money, sometimes known as seed funding or seed capital, is a form of securities offering in which an investor invests capital in a startup company in exchange for an equity stake or convertible note stake in the company.

After our meeting, I decided to lend Victor some money just to test things out. Instead of $5,000, I loaned him $2,000.

I'm sure you wouldn't be surprised to know that oftentimes the only thing that prevents people from growing their business is finances, especially if you're a young Black kid with no resources, and don't have any connections to banking or the investment world.

Victor's mom was ill and his father wasn't around. He was just a kid trying to make it and I wanted to help him by giving him a shot. But it wasn't for that reason only. The key things were that I believed in Victor's concept and I also believed in him.

I told Victor that I didn't want any interest back and that I was happy to help but had one condition. I wanted my money back within 60 days. We agreed, shook hands, and the next day I went to the bank to get the money for him.

Victor was on top of the world.

I'd see Victor at the YMCA every week after that and each week I'd ask him how sales were going. He'd say everything was running smoothly and that he'd have no problem paying me back within the 60-day timeframe that we agreed on. Unbeknownst to me, Victor was just playing it cool the entire time because within a month of me lending him the money, he walked into the YMCA, threw a big-ass Ziploc bag filled with $5 and $10 bills at me and said, "Yo, look at this, I told you I was the man!!!"

Victor was for sure a mini Trent in the making because that's exactly something I'd do. Maybe that's why I liked him so much.

Victor not only paid me back the $2000, he also put an extra $1000 in the bag and insisted that I take a profit. He wanted me to re-invest and come on as a partner, instead of just being nice and helping him out. That really impressed me.

Here was this little kid in high school, giving up $1000 because he saw the bigger picture. When starting a business, most people can't see past the money, their expenses or their profits. A CEO needs to be a visionary and to be able to look ahead 5-10 years down the line. What's a $1000 in profits when you can be making a million dollars in profits within a few years?

That's how true entrepreneurs think.

Regardless of Victor's offer, I didn't accept the $1000. I wanted him to keep it, but I did accept the other offer. I invested more seed money, and partner up with him.

. . .

A few nights later, I took Victor out and we talked about where he bought the Long Tees from and how he sold them. I asked him to explain to me his entire operation, from A to Z, and while doing so I quickly identified a huge problem. Victor was taking the bus to Plattsburgh, New York, a small American city that borders Montreal, and was buying Long Tees from a retail store for $7 USD. He sold them to kids in Montreal for $15 CAD. Those were horrible margins and one of the first things I knew we had to change if we wanted to be successful.

Margins are probably the most important keys to any business.

Margin:

*In business, **margin** refers to the difference between the seller's cost for acquiring products and their selling price. **Margins** for product sales appear as percentages of net sales revenues.*

*The profit **margin** is an accounting measure designed to gauge the financial health of a business or industry. In general, it is defined as the ratio of profits earned to total sales receipts (or costs) over some defined period.*

To buy Long Tees in the US, Victor had to convert his CAD (Canadian dollars) into USD (American dollars), which meant he was already taking a hit on the margins before even paying anything because the Canadian dollar is usually always weaker than the American dollar. We really had to find these Long Tees at a low price for the business to work.

Where do you go in the US to find a supplier when there is no distribution in Canada?

NEW YORK CITY, of course.

A few weeks after our meeting, we jumped into my Honda Accord and headed down the 87 South.

. . .

New York, August 2003

Our first stop in NYC was Canal St. and that's where we found some Tees for a bit less than $7.00 USD, but I knew we could do better. We needed to find wholesale prices.

What is a wholesale price?

*The **price** paid for large quantities of products, often from a wholesaler. Often purchased by businesses that will sell them on to the public at a higher retail **price**.*

I wanted to find out where the stores on Canal St. bought their merchandise but, of course, nobody would help us. We walked around for hours asking where we could find wholesale suppliers but we had no luck. It took us almost the entire day to find someone that finally gave us an idea of where we could go and look. We eventually found the place in Manhattan where all the local New York stores bought their merchandise. It was like discovering Wonderland!

It was an area of four blocks in the middle of Manhattan and you could literally find everything that you needed to open up a Hip Hop store, however I was only there to look for Long Tees and Du-Rugs, to start. Victor wanted to buy more but I just wanted to test things out and not bite off more than I could chew.

In this Hip Hop Wonderland, we finally found a supplier that sold Long Tees at wholesale prices. This place had so many tees it was ridiculous. They literally had over a million tees in stock and every colour, shade and size you could imagine -- XL to 8XL and even free size (which is basically a dress).

We had driven to New York in my two-door Honda Accord looking to bring back a few hundred tees to test the market, but this supplier had huge minimums. They were out of our league and didn't want to let us just buy a few hundred tees.

Suppliers that have minimums are typically businesses with low margins. They make a "minimum purchase requirement" to ensure that they make a certain amount of profit per transaction. Asking them to break their minimums will never go over well because you're cutting into profits, but I asked anyways.

I asked the sales rep if he could break the minimums for us but got a straight-up NO right away, but I knew that I'd get that answer. I only asked him so that he could say no and I could then turn around and say, "Can I speak to your manager or the owner, please?"

We had to wait an hour or so for the owner to be free, but he eventually met with us. I told him about our search to find him and how we ended up there. I also told him about Victor's story and how he started selling Long Tees in his high school, how Victor and I met, and about our plans to grow the business from the trunk of my car to a real legit brick-and-mortar retail store.

Brick & Mortar:

*The term **"brick-and-mortar"** refers to a traditional street-side business that offers products and services to its customers face-to-face in an office or store that the business owns or rents. The local grocery store and the corner bank are examples of **brick-and-mortar** companies.*

brick-and-mortar businesses sell products to customers in person *in a* physical location whereas **click-and-mortar** businesses take orders online, then deliver the products to the customer.

The name is a metonym derived from the traditional building materials associated with physical buildings: **brick and mortar**.

I told the owner that I would like to buy 500 tees and we had plans to not only hit his minimums in the near future but to also order way above his minimum orders within a few months. He smiled and tilted his head as if he couldn't believe that I just said 500 tees, but he didn't say no right away.

We continued to talk about a few other things and then after about 30 minutes or so he finally agreed to work with us. "I don't normally sell less then 2000 Long Tees per order, but I like you guys, and everyone needs help in the beginning," he said.

Our final agreement was for us to take 1000 Long Tees right away, but we'd have to buy another 1000 within the next 30 days, and then 2000 per month afterwards.

Victor was used to only buying and selling 200-300 tees at a time so buying 1000 tees at once was a risk. We didn't have the clientele yet to move that kind of quantity but at the prices we were now paying per tee, the risk was actually lower. The real risk was how the heck were we going to get 1000 Long Tees into my car and drive seven hours back to Montreal.

Our drive home was a fucking nightmare. It was so funny that I wish I had pictures of it. We stuffed my poor little Honda Accord to the max, the trunk, back seat, and in our laps. We didn't leave any empty space anywhere. Any place we could find to stuff a pack of shirts, we did. Till this day, I still don't know how we drove like that and made it back in one piece. I couldn't see out my rear-view mirror, or my side-mirrors.

. . .

Once we were back home in Montreal, I unpacked all of the tees at my dad's house and told Victor we'd hit up the high schools within the next few days. We had no time to waste. We had to move these tees quicker than we had originally planned since we had another 1000 to buy the next month.

Remember when I said that the risk of buying 1000 tees was actually lower than buying 300, let me explain why.

Not only did I negotiate our "order minimums" with our supplier, but I also negotiated the price. I got us a good deal. We paid $1.75 for each white tee, $2.25 each for a colour tee, and Du-Rags would be $0.33 each.

300 Tees @ $7.00 each (at the old supplier) = $2,100.00

1000 Tees @ $2.00 each (at the new supplier) = 2,000.00

We were basically paying the same price for three times more merchandise.

Do you also remember when I said margins are probably the most important key to any successful business, especially retail? The above example is the reason.

We sold our Long Tees for $10 each (lowered the price to make it more attractive and to sell more quickly) and Du-Rags were $5. You don't need me to show you those calculations to figure out how profitable we were; we were making bank!

I was excited and ready to take things to the next level.

. . .

We got to work very quickly and in a few weeks we had a tight little operation going. We had a "sales rep" in every high school in our area and they would bring their friends out at lunchtime or after school, and we'd give them free tees in return as pay. A few times teachers called the cops on us because they'd see two Black guys pull up in a black, fully tinted Honda Accord blasting Hip Hop music and would automatically assume we were up to no good. We'd try to tell them that we were just selling tees but they wouldn't believe us. They wanted us off the property.

We slowly moved away from schools and started selling in shopping centre parking lots, metro stations and doing home deliveries. My plans for being able to sell 2000 tees in a month were quickly met. We'd have to drive down to NYC every 2-3 weeks to keep up with demand. We never had too much inventory.

We sold Long Tees and Du-Rags from the trunk of my car for about four months, but driving around Montreal 3-4 days a week started to be a bit too much for us to handle. I didn't plan on things moving this quickly and I really wasn't sure what my next steps should be. Was it time to get a location or should I keep building my clientele and wait a bit longer? I had rented office space in the past for other business ventures but never a retail storefront space. I knew I had to be careful to keep our expenses to a minimum, plus I also wasn't sure how long this Long Tee craze was going to last. I didn't want to tie myself to anything long-term.

Over the next few weeks, I spent time looking around for places to rent, but then remembered I knew a tattoo shop in the area that had an empty space in the basement. I assumed that since it was in the basement rent would be cheap, and that the owner would love having us there because I could bring some extra attention to his shop. I drove by the shop and explained to the owner what I wanted to do and made him an offer.

At first, he said no right away without really letting me finish so he could explain to me that there was no way to operate a store from his basement. The ceiling was too low (6'5" high, I'm 6'2" btw) and there were no windows or cell phone reception, etc. It was more of a storage space than a legit basement.

When I heard his list of reasons for saying no, I couldn't have been happier. I knew that if I could convince him to say yes, that the rent would be low since he thought the space was so shitty. I was right. After a lot of back and forth, I was finally able to convince him to let me rent his 200-square-foot basement as is, and I'd pay him $300 a month. I told him we had a huge following already and we didn't need a traditional retail space with windows and a storefront. This would be better than selling tees from the trunk of my car. We would instantly bring a lot of attention to his shop and he could piggyback off of it. It was a win-win for both of us once I got him to see the entire picture.

. . .

Old-school business people will tell you business is all about location, location, and location. That's bullshit. It's all about product, product, and product.

Illegal drugs are sold throughout the world and is a thriving trillion-dollar business because the products are addictive.

"The money is always in the comeback!" #chrisrockvoice

Think of me as a legal drug dealer, the only difference between us is my product is legal and it doesn't kill people. Long Tees were my equivalent to crack.

If you're thinking of opening up a business or starting a brand, make sure you have the right product but don't sell drugs. That's not cool.

. . .

Now that we had somewhat of a real store, I decided to venture into other areas and diversify our brand. We started selling grills, earrings, watches, chains, jeans, and hoodies so that if Long Tees died down I'd still be able to pay the rent.

Diversify:

Diversification occurs when a business develops a new product or expands into a new market. Often, businesses diversify to manage risk by minimizing potential harm to the business during economic downturns. ... A business may also use diversification as a growth strategy.

While diversifying you have to make sure not to lose your customer. Walmart doesn't sell Louis Vuitton because that's not what their client base wants from them.

You can diversify your portfolio of businesses but you can't diversity too much within one business.

Diversify your portfolio/assets:

Diversification is the practice of spreading your investments around so that your exposure to any one type of asset is limited. This practice is designed to help reduce the volatility of your portfolio over time. ... One way to balance risk and reward in your investment portfolio is to diversify your assets.

Assets:

An asset is something containing economic value and/or future benefit. An asset can often generate cash flows in the future, such as a piece of machinery, a financial security, or a patent. Personal assets may include a house, investments or artwork.

I kept everything in the same vein as the Long Tees and Du-Rags. Most of our items were cheap and cost-effective; I wanted to be careful not to lose my base of high school kids. Most of them were buying from us using their pocket money or allowance. Most, if not all of the items in our store, were below $50 each and they were exclusive stuff you couldn't find in our area.

Yes, there were other Hip Hop stores in Montreal at the time, but none in the West Island around where we lived. The kids in our area would have to take public transportation 30-40 minutes into the city to shop for Hip Hop clothes so we were solving a problem. Also, if you ask me, the biggest difference between our shop and the others was **Victor.**

I'd do all the negotiations and business dealings, but Victor was the buyer. He knew what these kids really wanted and what they were into way before these other stores had a clue. Victor was a kid himself so he was also the client.

A couple months would pass before we got everything settled with our new location, new items, etc. It wasn't easy making that little basement look good but we pulled it together quite nicely. One man's trash is another man's treasure.

We were going from the trunk of a car so anything was better than that situation.

. . .

Montreal, February 2004

A few days before we opened, we had all of our "sale reps" come through for some snacks and drinks, and to also give them a sneak peek of the new store. We gave them some free stuff and asked them to tell all their friends about the opening.

It was a hit.

Opening day was amazing, and went off exactly as I planned. I think our clients were just happy to finally be able to come to us, instead of calling and waiting for us to come to them.

Although we now had an actual store, I made sure not to change that very personal relationship we had with our clients. My aim was to never lose what made us cool in the first place. I wanted the store to be a welcoming space before being a transactional space. Till this day, I still make sure every Exclucity location runs that same way. Today in our employee handbook, something that every staff member has to read and gets quizzed on, it tells the story of how the Exclucity brand began. It also emphasizes how important it is to me to keep that welcoming environment and vibe at every location.

As for Victor, he was in heaven. He was a 16-year-old kid making good money, working for himself, and doing something he loved. This guy started out taking the bus to the US to buy a few t-shirts to sell to his high school friends. Now, he was managing an up-and-coming Hip Hop store in Montreal. Good on him.

With everything finally set up and the store running smoothly, it was time for me to diversify **my** portfolio and shift my focus back to another business of mine, my management company.

Oh shit, I forgot to let you know about that.

. . .

It's said that most multimillionaires have up to six different revenue streams in their portfolio.

Revenue Streams:

A revenue stream is a source of revenue of a company or organization. In business, a revenue stream is generally made up of either recurring revenue, transaction-based revenue, project revenue, or service revenue.

One of the other businesses I was working on while building the store was a music management company. I had been managing my now ex-girlfriend's music career on the side (for support more than anything), but I really liked it and I thought I was good at it. I wasn't making any money from it, but music had always been my first love so that part of the job just came naturally to me.

The music industry has a lot of money, but more than the money music can open up a tremendous amount of other business ventures and revenue streams, which was the thing that excited me the most. Actually, at the time, I was only selling Long Tees and Du-Rags so I could build passive income to pay for my girlfriend's music career. Music was my main focus.

Passive Income:

*Passive income is earnings derived from a rental property, limited partnership, or any enterprise in which **a person is not actively involved**.*

Passive income is income that requires little to no effort to earn and maintain. It is called progressive passive income when the earner expends little effort to grow the income. Examples of passive income include rental income and any business activities in which the earner does not materially participate.

Passive income is how the richest among us still build their wealth*. When you don't have money, you can leverage your time and effort to create income streams that will grow into the future. As you accumulate money, you'll deploy that cash to make more and more passive income.*

I had developed a little buzz in the music industry, but that was just in Montreal. I knew if I wanted to make a name for myself, I needed to move to Toronto. Toronto also had a music management school that was very popular and I thought it could fast track my business and help me build some connections in the industry. I was excited for the opportunity and determined to make the move, but when I told my girlfriend about my plans, she didn't like the idea and had no interest in moving there with me.

As you may know by now, I don't let people or things stand in my way. When I'm focused on doing something, I'm usually going to do it regardless of the support. This doesn't apply to my girlfriend, but most people will tell you your ideas aren't good because they don't think they can do it, not because your ideas are bad. They are afraid of their failures so they put that on you. That's why I don't listen to most people.

I promise you that at some point, someone told Steve Jobs that his idea to make a phone with no buttons was a bad one. Imagine if he had listened to them.

The head offices of the five major Canadian record labels were in Toronto. How could moving there be a bad idea? I was very focused on making the move, despite my girlfriend's hesitation.

To make my decision easier, I met an Artists and Repertoire (A&R) representative from Universal Music who told me that I had real talent as a manager. He thought it was a good idea for me to move to Toronto. You can't tell a guy like me, an overly ambitious person, something like that and expect me to be still and complacent. That's all the push I needed to hear.

Complacent in business:

Complacency *is an intrinsic flaw that prevents organizations from pushing beyond the status quo to achieve exceptional successes. Avoiding **complacency** is essential to any **business's** long-term longevity.*

After a few weeks of looking deeper into things and finding a place to live, I officially made the decision to move to Toronto. I tried to convince my girlfriend to move with me because she never said my idea wasn't good. But she couldn't handle the uncertainly of it, which I understood. Our outlook on life was different and it was the uncertainty of the relocation that excited me the most. We were clearly on different paths. We discussed the option of a long-distance relationship, but I didn't think that was a good idea so we decided to breakup after a seven-year relationship. It was unfortunate because we had a good relationship. We were both of Jamaican descent, our parents knew each other before we got together, and our families were close but I knew it wouldn't work out. I was moving to Toronto and I was focused on one thing and one thing only - building an empire.

Once I was done with all my Toronto plans, I knew I had to get together with Victor and make some changes. I promised him that I'd come back from Toronto once every two weeks to take him to NYC and that I'd help him manage the store from Toronto. We didn't have much time to prepare because I had applied to the music management school and was accepted, and classes were starting in a few weeks. I really didn't have much to fear as all the groundwork at the store had been laid and a system built. All Victor had to do was follow it. What could go wrong?

What's the risk of me leaving a 16-year-old kid to run a Hip Hop store in the basement of a tattoo shop?

(I really don't know what I was thinking at the time. It was a complete nightmare).

. . .

Toronto, March 2004

From the first day I moved to Toronto, I was on top of the world. I was out every night meeting and connecting with new people. I surrounded myself with people in the music industry and we went out to clubs, concerts and showcases nightly. That was the huge advantage with the school. Not only were you learning, but the school also placed you smack in the middle of the Canadian music scene. You got to know and hang with all the right people.

During one of my nights out, I met a beautiful Bajan girl who literately captivated my entire world from the moment I met her. I was sprung! The best part of it was that she was in the music industry as well. She was an on-air radio personality.

Life in Toronto was amazing.

I would check in on Victor from time to time and all he'd say was everything was going well and we were good. I knew things couldn't be perfect but I was so focused on Toronto, music, and my new relationship that I just wanted to believe what he told me. I should have dug deeper than just asking a few questions.

Unfortunately (or maybe fortunately), in life you can only ignore and pretend that things are okay for so long before "the house" comes crashing down on you.

I started getting calls from my landlord saying that the basement was packed with teenagers smoking weed, drinking alcohol, and doing a bunch of foolishness. It started out as something that happened occasionally, but then quickly turned into a weekly routine. Not only did I have to deal with the landlord, but also the cash wasn't balancing and the daily counts were short.

My new girlfriend and I were working on some big things in the music industry, and things were really starting to take off for us. She was interviewing and making connections with some of the biggest names in the US Hip Hop game and I was out around town making a name for myself in the industry.

I had signed an amazing music artist/producer that I was 100% sure was going to blow up. In my head, I was about to make it big and I didn't have time to worry about Long Tees.

I was so busy in Toronto that I couldn't go back to Montreal as much and things started to be a real mess. With everything going on, I wasn't focused on the store at all anymore, and I slowly started to realize that without me being in Montreal overseeing everything it probably wouldn't last. It was already going downhill after a few months and was almost at a point of no return but deep down I didn't care because I had music.

I was at a crossroads! The plan of moving to Toronto and doing music was to build a second revenue stream, not replace one with the other. I was also very scared because if I closed the store, I'd have no revenue and no source of income. My management company was going great but I wasn't generating any profits yet.

Profits:

Profit is a benefit or gain, usually monetary. An example of profit is the money a business has left after paying their **expenses**.

*The simplest formula is: total revenue – total expenses = **profit***. *Profit is calculated by deducting direct costs, such as materials and labour and indirect costs (also known as overheads) from sales.*

People often mistake making money (revenue) with making profit. You can have sales of $10 million a year and make zero profit. Trust me, I know because it happened to me before. Even worse, you can sell $10 million and lose money; that has also happened to me.

Revenue:

*Revenue, also known simply as "**sales**", does not deduct any costs or expenses associated with operating the business. **Profit** is the amount of income that remains after accounting for all expenses, debts, additional income streams, and operating costs.*

Although I wasn't making any profits with my management company, I had a backup plan that would allow me to close the store and still be able to survive for a while.

I had a line of credit, a few credit cards, and some cash saved up. I calculated that I could make it through the next six months to a year, if I was careful. At the time I thought that was an amazing idea but now realize that was the stupidest thing I could have done.

. . .

Toronto, October 2004

Seven months after moving to Toronto, Victor had fucked up the store so much that we had no choice but to close it. I was so mad, I couldn't understand how that was possible, but I was also young and didn't know what I was doing.

I should have never left a 16-year-old kid to run a store all by himself. Even if it was a small store in a basement, a teenager needs proper supervision and guidance. I realized that now and I know that it was my mistake, not his.

Regardless of what I know now, at the time I was PISSED and didn't even go down for the closing of the store. I loved Victor like a little brother but he was basically stealing money from me, so I couldn't work with him anymore. I told Victor we were done and not to call me ever again.

Victor makes a second appearance in my life a few years later, when I decided to reopen the store and hire him. But before I get to that part of the journey, let me quickly tell you what happened to my management company in Toronto. Drake is in the story for like five minutes, it's a good one.

. . .

Soldier Management

Closing the store was horrible, but on the positive side of things, there was nothing pulling me back to Montreal anymore. I could now focus 100% on my management company.

While I was out at an event one night, I met a woman who was opening a small boutique management company and was looking for an intern. Tyra had just left her job at a major management company that had among its clients Nelly Furtado, who at the time was huge. She was an older woman, who was married with children, and was looking for a business partner that was young and in the streets. I was the cool kid from Montreal that knew all the DJs and had all the connections to people in the city, and my girlfriend was the co-host of the hottest Hip Hop radio show at the time. Tyra and I were a perfect match for each other.

Tyra had years of experience and knew all the hands-on things that I needed to learn about music management. I could learn way more interning for her than I ever could at the school.

Most of what they taught at the school, I was already doing on my own. One of the big selling points of the school was that the professors were in the industry. But within a few months of being in Toronto, I was getting into events and hanging in circles that my professors weren't. At this point, the school was a waste of time and money for me.

I was bored; I needed a bigger challenge so I decided to leave.

. . .

Toronto, February 2005

A year after moving to Toronto, I was still riding high, everything was going as planned. I had it all except for one thing…. I HAD NO MONEY COMING IN!!!

My line of credit and credit cards were maxed out and I had no more cash saved up. I thought my credit and cash would last longer than they did. But money doesn't last long in a big city like Toronto when you have rent to pay and you're going out every night, buying drinks and socializing. You can't live that kind of lifestyle with zero income and I really didn't know what to do.

I started feeling like I had screwed up and was in a rut that I couldn't get myself out of. Thinking back now, yes, I could have given up my management dreams and gotten a job. But in my head, I was so close to making it big and making money that I couldn't just stop.

I tried my best to make things work, but unfortunately, one night I hit rock bottom and I knew I needed help.

One Saturday night in the middle of winter, I was out at a club with my girlfriend and we got into an argument. I don't remember what it was about, but she got pissed off, left the club and went home. I stayed for a little while longer but then decided to go home. It was freezing, windy and snowing outside. I jumped into a cab but before the driver could ask me where I was going, I immediately sobered up and said to myself, "Trent, how the fuck are you going to pay for this cab?" My cards were maxed out and I had no idea if I had enough money in my bank account to pay with my debit card.

I jumped out of the cab and ran a few blocks to the closest bank machine. I tried to withdraw $60 and it displayed "insufficient funds."

Then I tried $40 and the same thing happened. I took a deep breath, keyed in $20, closed my eyes and just prayed that I'd hear that little noise you hear when the machine starts counting your money but no luck. There was no noise, there was just silence, and I knew what that meant.

I opened my eyes and all I saw was "insufficient funds."

It turned out that I only had $3.52 in my bank account, which was not even enough to get me down the street. My girlfriend had been paying everything for us for the past couple of months, and she also paid for everything that night at the club. I could have taken a cab home and she would have paid the fare, but I had too much pride.

I tucked my pants into my socks, pulled my sleeves down over my hands, put my hands over my ears and began my long walk home. It took me approximately one and a half hours to get home. I literally couldn't feel parts of my body when I got there.

After months of living off my line of credit and credit cards and just scraping by, then months of not being able to make ends meet and having no money at all, I made the very difficult call to the welfare office and set up an appointment. I filled out an application form and started receiving welfare.

Before writing this book, I had never told a single soul about being on welfare. It was, and still is, the lowest point ever in my life.

. . .

Toronto, May 2005

I needed to clear my head. It was time for me to get my life in order.

I needed to start making some money fast so the first thing I did was to quit interning with Tyra. Things weren't going well with my girlfriend so I broke up with her.

I moved out of my girlfriend's apartment and I rented a very small 10x10 attic apartment on Dufferin Street in Toronto for $400 a month. That was the worst place I ever lived in my life. There were six bedrooms in the house, four on the main and second floor and two rooms in the attic. The kitchen and bathroom were all shared, and there was no den, basement, living room, or dinning room. Those were all converted into bedrooms. There were six grown men living in this small house that hadn't been renovated in about 30 years and it seemed to have not been cleaned for just as long. It was so gross but it was all I could afford at the time. Luckily, for some odd reason my room was the only one in the house that had a sink and I never had to use the shared bathroom. To shower, I went to the YMCA down the street every day, and I was good.

Oh, and the place was infected with mice.

I tried my hardest to never be home or talk to anyone with whom I shared the house. I'd leave at 8 a.m. and come back late at night just to sleep and that was it.

I was in a bad place. I had nothing back in Montreal and now I had nothing in Toronto either. Everything that was so good had just come to a screeching halt. It's like I was in a movie and someone hit the stop button, or like I was dreaming and someone had just woken me up.

Of course, I know now that it was my fault and that I had been making some really stupid decisions. But that's all part of business, right? You almost have to go through those things to get where you're going, at least that's the way I looked at it, anyways.

Determined to fix things and pull myself back up, I opened a new management company called Soldier Management. It didn't make money right away but it could once I found the right artists.

While I was building my new management company and looking for artists to work with, I knew that I had to make some money on the side so I started modelling, acting, and doing some background work on TV and movies being filmed in Toronto. (Watch "Cheaper by the Dozen 2" very closely.)

From the outside looking in, everything was great. From what people saw, I had moved to Toronto a year ago, went to school, interned at a management company, linked up with the biggest people in the Toronto music industry, dated the hottest girl in the city, and now I was on my own starting my management company. No one had a clue that I was on welfare, showering at the YMCA, in debt and was doing background extra work just so that I could survive.

Remember that next time you see someone on Instagram acting like his or her life is so great; things aren't always what they seem.

. . .

Toronto, August 2005

Over the next couple of months things were just okay, I was barely scraping by but I was able to stay afloat. Soldier Management was off the ground and within a few months things started to get better for me.

There was a Hip Hop group that I had known about from back in the day in Montreal. One of its members was thinking about putting out a solo project. The group had already released an album but members thought they'd have a better shot at success if the leader put out his solo album next.

Their group album had some success but it was only locally and it wasn't profitable. With this new solo project they wanted to ensure that they sold nationally so that they could recoup and be more lucrative. They thought it best to hire someone from Toronto to help execute that national plan.

Recoup:

To get back an amount of money you have lost or spent.

I met with the group in Montreal and liked their ideas, their plans and the artist that they wanted to launch. More importantly, they had their own independent label and they had a budget to work with. I believed we had a good shot at being successful.

Being in the tough money situation that I was in, I set up my new management company a bit differently than a traditional management company would, or even the standard way they taught us in school. Typically, a manager takes a percentage of the artist's earnings, which means if the artist isn't making any money then neither are you. Instead of managing artists, I flipped it and started managing independent record labels that had artists. I took 15% of what the label was spending on their artists. I would act as the artist's manager to the public, but in reality I was really working for the record label.

I signed a deal with the guys from Montreal for a $100,000 project; which meant I made $15,000 upfront right away. When you're young, broke and eating one meal a day, $15,000 sounds more like $150,000.

I was ecstatic.

Signing that deal was the most stressful thing I ever had to do. I acted like it was nothing to me, but the truth was I needed the money more than anyone would have ever known. As soon as we signed the deal and I got my cheque, I went straight to the bank that day and completely paid off all my credit cards and put the rest on my line of credit.

I kept some money for myself because I had to go shopping. My clothes were starting to look worn out and I needed a new pair of shoes badly.

· · ·

Over the next few months, I drove back and forth between Montreal and Toronto two to three times a week for meetings, photo shoots and studio sessions. We worked really hard and put together a solid album that I thought would do great. It wasn't exactly how I wanted it, which was to be more mainstream and commercial, but we still had a good project.

After the album was done, I brought the guys to Toronto and introduced them to all the right people. We played the album for a lot of the top DJs, radio stations, producers and artists in the city.

My industry friends in the city liked the project and thought we had a good album with two or three solid singles. With the help of my friends in the industry, we picked our first single and decided to shoot a video.

· · ·

Toronto, June 2006

Within one year of starting my new management company, I had signed a new artist, recorded and completed an album, and had his new single playing on radio stations across the county with the music video on heavy rotation on Much Music. (That's when music videos actually played on TV. lol). I was really starting to make a name for myself in the industry as a professional manager that gets shit done.

I was doing big things, and people were starting to notice it.

One night in Toronto, I was coming out of a club and someone recognized me and said, "Hey, you're the guy who manages that rapper from Montreal, right?" He continued, "I saw your video on Much Music, I like that song and I like what you guys are doing out here." I replied, "Ya, that's us. Thanks a lot, man." At the time I had no idea who I was talking to, but it was DRAKE.

Drake then wasn't the Drake of today, he had only put out a few songs but there was no huge buzz. "Replacement Girl" with Trey Songz hadn't come out yet. We were on the same level and even using the same video production company for our videos. I hadn't really heard much of his music so I had no idea that I was talking to an artist that shared a similar vision. His sound was exactly what I was looking for before I signed my artist. It was very lyrical, Hip Hop but also extremely radio friendly, commercial and mainstream. He's a manager's dream artist.

You'd think it's an easy mix for an artist to have all of those things but it's not, its extremely difficult and rare to find. That's why Drake is Drake and he may never be duplicated.

Anyways after talking outside the club, we exchanged numbers but neither of us ever called each other.

Stupid me.

We'd meet up again a year or so later while we were shooting a video but this time when we did he was a celebrity. There was no let's chop it up and talk about music. He showed up to the video set to see someone from the production company, stole all the energy out of the room, and everyone was excited that Drake was there. Our video vixen, Summer Walker, (not the artist, the video vixen) was supposed to be on set but she was all chatty, chatty, with Drake and delayed our shit. I think they actually started dating after that or something. I'm not sure.

The moral of the story is, always follow up with people you meet. You never know who's going to be the next international superstar rapper.

. . .

Anyways, back to the journey.

My artist didn't break internationally like Drake did, but we still had some great Canadian success and that's what I was paid to do. We released three singles on radio that got national airplay and the music videos that we shot for the singles were played on heavy rotation on Much Music. That was a huge accomplishment coming from an unknown artist and a startup management company. It's something that I'm still proud of till this day.

The label was very happy with my work and decided to continue pushing the album and working with me. They asked me to put together another $100,000 budget but this time it was going to be for a Canadian promo tour. I put a proposal together and they approved it right away, which meant I got another $15,000 cheque, which is exactly the amount I needed to be completely debt-free.

I did the same thing that I did the last time I received a cheque. From the contract signing, I went straight to the bank and deposited my money. I put $10,000 on my line of credit, and boom just like that, I was free of all my debts and had some leftover change.

. . .

I went from being on welfare and having all of my credit maxed out to having a profitable company, getting off welfare and being debt-free in about one year; all because I never gave up. I know how corny it sounds but I don't think people understand what "not giving up" truly means. Not giving up is the single most difficult thing you'll ever have to do in life and in business.

For me, not giving up meant sleeping in an attic during the summer and having to return my futon to IKEA every three months and to buy it back so that I had something to sleep on. Sure, I could have given up and lived comfortably at one of my parents' home or even at my sister's house. I had a way out but I didn't take it.

Giving up is never an option for me.

. . .

Victor – Part 2

Montreal, August 2006

Throughout all of my ups and downs in Toronto, I always knew that things would have been much better if the store back in Montreal was still up and running. I was still pissed off at Victor, but it had been two years and I knew that it wasn't entirely his fault. On top of that, I had heard from some people in Montreal that Victor had completely changed. People told me that he had turned to religion, found God, and was a changed man.

I really wanted to reopen the store again but I knew I needed Victor's help to execute it properly. Regardless of our past, business is business and sometimes you've got to work with people that you have issues with. It's best to try and work out those differences than to let a good business go to waste.

I had cleared off all of my debt and I had some extra cash lying around in the bank. Some people will tell you savings or TSFA accounts are good, and they are, but saving accounts just aren't for me. I like when my money is out working for me, making me more money.

Investing:

An **investment** is an asset or item acquired with the goal of **generating income or appreciation**. ... For example, an investor may purchase a monetary asset now with the idea that the asset will provide income in the future or will later be sold at a higher price for a profit.

Investing is the act of allocating resources, usually money, with the expectation of generating an income or profit. You can **invest** in endeavours, such as using money to start a business, or in assets, such as purchasing real estate in hopes of reselling it later at a higher price.

I still wasn't 100% sure what I should do about Victor and the store. But one day I was back in Montreal visiting my family and I bumped into a mutual friend of ours. He told me that Victor wanted to reach out to me for a while now, but was nervous to do so because he had heard how mad I was at him. This friend suggested that I call Victor, hear him out, and see how things go. I thought why not, maybe it was a good idea.

I called Victor and we spoke on the phone for a bit and things went well. He told me that he also wanted to call me for the past few months but never did and was happy that I called. He invited me over to his apartment for a drink so we could talk. I said yes and we decided to meet up a few days later.

When Victor and I met up it was like I was looking at a completely different person. He was shaven, clean-cut and he was in the process of removing all his tattoos.

Church had done him well.

I opened up to him about how disrespected and betrayed I felt over what he did. I asked him to just be honest with me about what really happened to the money and inventory when I left and moved to Toronto.

Victor was honest. He told me that he lied about some of the days being off but he also said that it was friends that he allowed to hang out with him who stole from the store. At the time, he didn't want to rat them out so he just played dumb and didn't say anything about it because he knew I'd go off. He also said that he didn't take anything seriously and was really immature back then.

I told Victor that while I hated feeling betrayed I also felt like more of the blame should have been on me as the leader. I left him with a lot of responsibility and no accountability. Calling in once in a while and not showing interest was irresponsible and would have caused a divide.

We spoke for a few hours, reminisced on the good times and both agreed that we were a great team and had left a lot of money on the table. There was no reason why we couldn't open back up the store and make it work even better this time.

While I agreed to work with Victor again, I did make it clear that it would be totally different this time. This would be MY store, run by me and me only. I'd pay him well but I needed to make all the rules and final decisions. He'd just be an employee this time.

Without hesitation, Victor said yes. He was not only happy to get a second chance to redeem himself but Victor was also going through a very tough time financially. He didn't have enough money for food and I think that's why he suggested having our meeting at his place. He wanted me to see his situation.

I think he was hiding it from everyone. I felt really bad for him so I took him out to get some groceries and gave him $300 for pocket money.

I told Victor that I needed a few weeks to sort out some things but promised him I'd try to get things started soon so I could help him get back on his feet.

. . .

I was about to head out across Canada on a promo tour with my artist and the label, so I asked Victor if he was down to take a quick drive down to New York with me before I left to touch base with our suppliers, and he said yes, he would come.

It was on this trip that I was stopped at the border, and found out I was BANNED FROM ENTERING THE UNITED STATES OF AMERICA, and we had to cancel the trip.

This put my entire plan of re-opening the store in jeopardy.

. . .

I'll get into more detail in Trent 2 | Young, Dumb & Ignorant about my past troubles, but after finding out that I needed to apply for a US Entry Waiver that is only issued by the United States Department of Homeland Security and that it takes 6-8 months to get approved, IF you get approved, I literarily had a panic attack. I was freaking out and had to seriously reconsider my plans of opening back up the store. How could I own a store that sells exclusive product from the US if I couldn't even enter the country?

I was in a scramble to figure things out and I needed to make a decision on what to do since I was leaving for tour in a few weeks. My biggest issue was that Victor didn't have a license yet so I had to find someone that would drive him down to New York for me every month. But who the heck was going to do that and not charge me a fortune to do it.

After a while, I remembered that I knew a girl who had lost her job. I was sure she'd be willing to do it for me for free. Perhaps maybeeeeee she liked me so I played on that a bit, but don't judge me, OK. I was in a tight spot, lol! I gave her money to buy some things in New York for herself, she was happy to do it.

After that little bump in the road was solved, I had everything pretty much cleared up and I was ready to go. Victor was dialed in, I had the cash, we had a driver but there was still one thing missing, we needed a store.

I knew it wasn't going to be easy to get our old landlord to trust us again, and that if I asked he'd probably say no, but I called him and tried anyway because I knew how to deal with him. I simply told the landlord that I really wanted the basement back and I'd be willing to pay double my previous rent. His NO turned into a yes within seconds. Of course, because of what happened last time the landlord put a tonne of restrictions and rules that Victor had to follow. But I told him that things would be completely different this time and that he had nothing to worry about. My rules would be stricter than his.

. . .

I was going to be on tour for six weeks which was way more than enough time for Victor to go back to New York, pick up the inventory and get everything ready for when I got back.

Within two months of getting out of debt, I had everything lined up and was ready to open my new store. I was so excited. It was a classic full circle moment.

I set a grand opening date for Oct 21, 2006.

. . .

Across Canada, September 2006

Going on tour with a rapper that has a song on the radio and a video in heavy rotation is hands down the most fun you'll ever have in your life. Every night is a full-fledged party. Every night you're in a new city, a new club and then you move on to a new province and do it all over again.

As much fun as it was going out on tour, it was still a job. As the manager, I had to make sure everything was organized, running smoothly and on time. I made it look easy because I was up partying late at night, but while everyone slept in, I was up early in the morning organizing everything for the day and made sure we stuck to the schedule.

Regardless of my many sleepless nights and very busy days, I still called Victor every day, sometimes multiple times per day, just to make sure everything was running smoothly and that we were sticking to the schedule. Most of the groundwork was done before I left but I needed to make sure. I wasn't going to have a repeat of the first time.

The tour went by very quickly and after six long weeks of being on the road, doing radio, club dates, shows and partying every night, I was just happy to make it home and to be alive. The first thing I did when I got home was to head straight to the doctor to get 14 HIV and STD tests, lol. I still thank the Lord today that I got a clean bill because every night on the tour was wild.

I wish I could have stayed in bed for a month after that tour as I really needed to recover, but sleep wasn't an option. I had a store to open.

. . .

Montreal, October 2006

On October 21, 2006, Exclucity (Hip Hop Exclusive) was officially born. I'll explain the name change later.

I was OFFICIALLY BACK.

I couldn't have been happier. Everything was finally running smoothly again. The landlord was happy, our clients were happy that we were back, but there was one person who wasn't.

Victor!

Even though Victor and I had been speaking daily and he was happy to be making money again, he was conflicted. Having made a 180-degree change in his life, that also trickled down to the type of music that

Victor listened to, the clothes he wore, and everything else that interested him.

He had found religion and didn't want me playing Hip Hop music in the store anymore, nor did he want me selling jewelry, grills or baggy clothes. According to Victor, everything that we were selling was the devil's plan and it was the devil working through us.

The problem I had was this, why was Victor only telling me this now a few months after we opened? Why now after he has a few bucks in his pocket? Maybe Victor didn't change, maybe he just got more cunning in his ways.

I was pissed and didn't know what to do but I wasn't going to let it get me down. This was my store, and it was my problem to solve. I had tried my best to work with Victor as much as I could, but things didn't last more than two months with him. He wanted out and he quit.

Since the day Victor left, I have not seen or spoken to him. He reached out to me a few times but kick me once shame on you, kick me twice, shame on me.

. . .

Halftime Update
Montreal, December 2006

Ok, at this point in my journey, I had a few revenue streams going and they were all running smoothly.

Let me recap them.

1) Soldier Management was up and running with a successful artist with music out, and I had just signed a new artist that had big national plans.

2) Modelling -- mainly in Toronto.

3) Became a member of the union, ACTRA (Alliance of Canadian Cinema, Television and Radio Artists), and designated a professional actor. Had a permanent background role on an ABC series being shot in Toronto.

4) Hip Hop Exclusive store, which brought in the most money of all my revenue streams.

Things were great, but Victor's leaving really put everything at risk because if I had to work at the store that would mean I'd be tied down in one place for too long. I needed to always be on the move. During those times I think I drove back and forth between Montreal and Toronto about three times per week and it is a five-hour drive. Irrespective of how hard I was willing to work, I couldn't physically do all of that and work at the store.

As you can imagine, things started falling apart.

I immediately had to stop doing background work, which paid me $25 per hour, 8 hours per day, plus 4 hours overtime each day. That was hard to let go but I knew it wasn't part of my dream. It was just a cash grab to help me get by but my problems didn't end there.

To make matters worse, the record label that I had just toured with started acting shady. They had all my contacts in the industry and were doing things behind my back so that they wouldn't need to pay me my 15% commission, which was such an amateurish move. My connections are just that, MY connections, and the first thing they did was to call me.

Yeah, sure they might take your job, but they aren't gonna work with you the same way if I'm not in the picture. Your experience isn't going to be the same without me being involved. Plus, you're not only paying for my connections, you're paying for my vision and guidance. I quickly cut ties and dropped them right away. That's why I won't mention the name of the artist in this book. I'm not giving any of them any SHINE!

#yesiknowiampetty

I would go on to sign a few more new artists and make some money, but the store and modelling were still my biggest moneymakers over the next year.

My revenue streams went from four down to two in the blink of an eye, but that's the point of having multiple streams, when one stops, you still have others to fall back on.

Furthermore, the best part of having multiple streams of income is you're never at the mercy of one person or situation. You can say FUCK YOU without fear to the people that do you dirty and that feeling of independence is addictive.

It keeps you hustling.

. . .

Doing It on My Own
Montreal, Jan. - Oct. 2007

With Victor gone, I was left to do everything at the store on my own, but at the same time I was happy about it. I knew the store could be a huge asset if I built it properly, and I was happy that it was in my hands only to manage.

I'd open and close the store daily, manage the clients alone, and I even went to New York by myself to pick up inventory. I'd close the store for one day, drive to New York, pick up the inventory and come right back that same day.

I also decided to change things up a bit and started bringing in a broader assortment of clothes. Still very Hip Hop, but I included polo shirts, jogging suits, denim, and every colour Dickies you could ever imagine. I even introduced some women's clothing.

Lastly, one of the most important things I decided to do was to make a yearly budget plan to make sure I was profitable over the next year. That's a must for a startup. Every penny counts in the beginning and one of the most important things is to stay on budget.

Budget in business:

*A **budget** is a detailed **plan** that outlines where you'll spend your money monthly or annually. You give every dollar a "job", based on what you think is the best use of your **business** funds, and then go back and compare your **plan** with reality to see how you did.*

*A **business budget** provides an accurate picture of expenditures and revenues and should drive important **business** decisions such as whether to increase marketing, cut expenses, hire staff, purchase equipment, and improve efficiencies in other ways.*

Why is it important to follow a budget?

*Since **budgeting** allows you to create a spending plan for your money, it ensures that you will always **have** enough money for the things you need and the things that are **important** to you. Following a **budget** or spending plan will also keep you out of debt or help you work your way out of debt if you are currently in debt.*

One key thing about savings is that most people don't realize that savings on small things add up to big saves in the end, like driving to New York, for example. Driving back and forth between Montreal and NYC on the same day is extremely hard to do, but it's a huge money saver. There was no hotel room to pay for and less expenses like food, etc. When you spread that out over a year, it really adds up. I still remember my routine like it was yesterday. I'd wake up at 2 a.m. and I'd try to be in NYC by 10 a.m. I'd have all my inventory picked, paid and packed in the minivan by 2 p.m., and be heading back to Montreal to try and be at the store before the landlord closed at 9 p.m. since I didn't have a key. It was a very long day with the most difficult part being the long lines at the border. Because I had a waiver now, I had to cross the border in the waiver line, which meant the process was even longer.

(OH SHIT!!!! HOLD UP!!! I forgot to tell you, I FINALLY GOT MY WAIVER!)

When Victor quit on me, I had no idea how I was going to get my inventory, but my waiver came in the mail a few weeks later. God always has a plan and things usually work out the way they are supposed to.

Anyways, back to the story.

So yes, I worked at the store every day for about a year by myself. I'd get help from my cousin here and there, but for the most part I was alone in that small basement, 11:30 a.m. to 9 p.m., 7 days a week. I really had things functioning well, business was good and I knew it was time for me to get some permanent help if I wanted to eventually get out of the store.

. . .

Montreal, November 2007

At the YMCA where I volunteered, the same one that I met Victor, there was a girl working at the front desk whose name was Peaches. She was a very nice person who got along with everyone and I thought she'd be a good fit to work at the store.

Peaches and I would always chat about the store. She'd always ask me how it was going and told me that if I ever needed some extra help to just let her know. She was willing to work a few hours per week as she was looking for a second job to make some extra cash.

Knowing that I had Peaches wanting to work for me and I still had my cousin, Sandra, willing to help me out on odd days, I thought maybe I should go back into modelling full-time again. Over the year, I still took a few gigs here and there but nothing major because I was so focused on building the store.

Although I hated aspects of modelling, such as looking into a camera and smiling for six hours a day, which is mind-numbing; I liked the opportunities it could bring me. It wasn't about the money, instead, it was about revenue streams that modelling and fame could open up for me. That's what was enticing.

Jay Z didn't become a billionaire off rap. He used rap to become a billionaire.

With that, I called up my modelling agency and told them I was interested in coming back. I told them that I got my life in order and my business was back on track. I was willing to take another crack at it again, but this time I wanted things to be different.

I wanted my agency to start pushing me outside of Montreal and Toronto to the international market. With the store running so well, if I was going to take my attention away from it, I wanted it to be worth it and I felt like it was my time.

When I first started modelling, I was signed to a small starter agency in Montreal. After a year, I left them for a better agency, and from there a few years later I got signed to Elite Model Management, which is arguably the biggest modelling agency in the world. I had already done the legwork and paid my dues so I was ready for the big leagues.

My agency was happy to have me back, but I had to work to get myself back to where I was before. I'm no stranger to hard work and was ready for it.

Fun Fact:

I got into modelling because of Alicia Keys. When I first met her she thought I was a model. I figured if Alicia Keys thinks I look good enough to be a model, I'm gonna start modelling.

. . .

Montreal, December 2007

I don't know if it was just a coincidence but right around the time I started modelling again and wasn't at the store as much my landlord called me. "Soooooooooooo, I heard you're back modelling, things are going well for you," he said. Right away, I knew where this was going. He continued, "You've been here for over a year now and most days your store is busier than mine. I'm going to be raising your rent starting next month."

Unfortunately, he had the right to do that because I had no lease, which meant I had no leg to stand on. I was at his mercy.

Side note: *Regardless of how you're feeling, when you're negotiating with someone the worst thing you can do is let the other person know that they are affecting you.*

Remaining calm, I said, " I understand rents go up but you have to give me warning and some time to plan for it all." I then followed up with, "Let's sit down, make an actual lease, and agree on yearly rental increases. That's the way it's supposed to be done, let's do it properly."

I wasn't really worried about this initial raise in the rent. I had been there for a year so it was fair. But I wanted to protect myself from him raising the rent in the future whenever he felt like it.

He quickly replied, "No, sorry, I want $1,500 per month, starting next month and I'm not giving you a lease."

Right then and there, I knew exactly what was going on. When your landlord gives you that kind of counteroffer, he's not looking to negotiate with you; he's trying to kick you out.

At first, I couldn't figure out his reason. I thought maybe he had someone else coming to rent the place but then I put two and two together. He wanted me out so he could open a store of his own. I had made that location into a hotspot and he wanted to capitalize off of it.

Imagine that! This guy had an empty basement for like 5 years doing nothing with it, collecting NO money, but now he wanted to be greedy and open up his own shop. I guess that's business, but still that's just dirty.

As soon as I figured out what he was doing, I started making plans to get out of there quickly so he wouldn't have time to set up a store and piggyback off of my success. If the store remained empty for a long period of time, he'd never be able to bring back the hype that I created. I no longer thought about ways to keep my business alive, I only thought about ways to bury his business before it even began.

I'm a Cancer, my level of petty is 50 Cent level, maybe worse. Lol!

I never gave him a decision on the rent increase. I told him I'd think about the $1,500 to give myself some time to get out of there without him knowing.

It was the end of December, liquidation season, so I decided to have a crazy Boxing Day sale to get rid of my inventory quickly, and it worked. Actually, it worked a little too well.

One day, my landlord saw how low my inventory was and asked me what was going on. All I told him was that I was really busy and hadn't gotten a chance to go to New York yet, which was a complete lie.

A few weeks passed, it was mid-January and he came downstairs again and asked, "What's up man? The store is almost empty, what are you doing? ". I replied, "This is going to be my last week here. I'll be closing this Sunday. Thank you for the opportunity."

It felt so good walking out of there and still gives me joy today. That was such a boss move on my part, just leaving like that and knowing I totally fucked up all his plans. It makes me very happy.

I heard he tried calling Victor to come and help him run a store down there but that didn't work out. Victor wasn't about that life anymore. I also heard he tried to sell some whack ass no name t-shirts and jeans down there but that didn't work either. It's not about the location. It's always about the product, ALWAYS THE PRODUCT.

The product that I sold in that basement wasn't available anywhere else in the West Island of Montreal. That's the only reason why people would shop in the basement of a tattoo parlour with low ceilings and no windows.

Not only did my landlord not have the right product but kicking me out brought him bad karma, that store was doomed before it even began.

If you don't believe in karma or energy, I suggest reading *The Alchemist* by Paulo Coelho. You will never have true success if you're a bad person. You might have some success for a short time, but trust me somehow karma will always come back and bite you in the ass.

Fourteen years after my landlord kicked me out of that basement and jeopardized my entire business for his own selfish reasons, I'm still standing strong. I've become a self-made multimillionaire and Exclucity is a national brand with global recognition. My landlord's store in the basement never got off the ground and his tattoo shop is now closed.

Karma just isn't a bitch. Karma is a FULL-ON RELENTLESS ASSHOLE.

Be a good person!

. . .

Montreal, January 2008

My main goal in life was to have MULTIPLE STREAMS OF INCOME and closing the store meant I was left with just one – modelling – which happened to be the least profitable at the time.

So here I was at home contemplating what the fuck I should do with my life. Yes, I had money in the bank and a modelling career, but no artist signed to my management company and no store. It wasn't looking good for me, AGAIN!

Looking back at this time in my life now is so overwhelming. It seemed every six months something would alter the next six months; it was crazy. I don't know why I didn't give up at some point, but I think that's the reason why I always say drive and ambition are things that school can't teach you, they are either in you or not. And if you ask me, it's one of the most essential aspects of business or self-employment.

Things will undoubtedly get extremely taxing but you cannot break.

Even though the store had gotten bigger and more popular, I still had most of my clients' phone numbers or MSN and still kept in contact with them when I closed the store. They would constantly badger me to find out if I was going to open back up a new location or drive around to high schools and their houses again. Either way, they just wanted me back in business.

I was not gonna drive around to high schools again, but I also knew that I was missing out on a lot of the money if I didn't open another store soon. One night, I was at home watching the crime film, *American Gangster*, and came up with a brilliant idea!!!!

In *American Gangster*, Denzel Washington's character, Frank Lucas, is a drug dealer who gets fed up with his New York drug connection and decides to go to Vietnam to buy his drugs from "the source." Then I thought, why the fuck don't I do that???

A friend had just moved to China to teach English and I knew 80% of the things that I sold at the store were made in China. I asked myself, why don't you go to China, find the source and start manufacturing your own goods? I had nothing else better to do as I was just sitting at home so I decided to seize the opportunity and go there to try to find "the source."

I called my friend in China, booked a flight and I was out the next week. I swear at the time, I thought this was the most brilliant idea in the world. I really didn't know what I was thinking.

. . .

China, End of January 2008

Before going to see my friend in Shanghai, I stopped for a few days in Guangzhou and it was there that I actually found the REAL "Hop Hip Wonderland." It was one hundred times bigger than the one I found in Manhattan, New York. It took me a few days to find it and it was crazy.

Shortly after finding that area, my brilliant idea came to a crashing halt. Factories out there would only work on minimums orders, and not that kind of minimums that I was used to in New York. I mean REAL minimums. They needed orders in the 20,000 – 30,000 units per order.

I stuck around there for a few more days just learning and soaking things up, but then I quickly jumped back on a plane and headed to Shanghai to meet up with my friend.

After spending a few days in Shanghai, we went to four other provinces in China looking for factories that would accept smaller orders, but I knew from my week in Guangzhou that it was never going to happen.

The silver lining in the story is that one factory that I visited gave me samples of some earrings to bring back with me, hoping I'd place an order with them in the future. They gave me 200 studded earrings (which is nothing to them) and I'd later sell them in my store for $20 each. Those 200 earrings alone paid for a big chunk of my trip.

After my failed trip to China, I knew my idea of being a manufacture/wholesaler was never going to happen, which only left me one option. If I wanted to stay in the fashion industry, it was going to be in retail, which meant I'd have to find a new location and reopen the store.

What's the difference between Wholesale & Retail?

*The primary difference between **wholesale** and **retail** is that the former is a business-to-business model and the latter a business-to-consumer model. In a **wholesale** model, you don't sell products directly to consumers. ... In a retailing model, you obtain products from a distributor and sell products directly to consumers.*

Is wholesale better then retail?

***Wholesale** can provide you with more stability because the responsibility for selling your product to consumers by-and-large falls to the **wholesale** buyer. **Wholesaling** also comes with fewer expenses, at least when compared to the money spent year-round on in-store marketing and standard **retail** overhead.*

Why are wholesale prices cheaper then retail prices?

*The reason the **wholesale** price is so much **cheaper than retail** price is because the **retailer** is providing a service to the consumer. That service may be knowledge of the products, the **retail** location, accessibility, or a wide variety of other things that make it easier for customers to gain access to certain products.*

If I was going to open back up the store, I wanted to do it properly and aim for something much bigger. I had paid my dues and earned the right to have a legit store. It had to be a storefront with windows, cell phone reception, and not be in a basement.

I think I was at a point in my life when I decided to demand more of myself, like I did in modelling with my request for international jobs. There comes a time in life when you have to tell yourself and the world that you're ready for the next level, and you have to say goodbye to whoever doesn't believe in you or tries to hold you back.

Self-Confidence:

Confidence comes from a Latin word 'fidere' which means "to trust"; therefore, having self-confidence is having trust in one's self.

Self-confidence *is an attitude about your skills and abilities. It means you accept and trust yourself and have a sense of control in your life. You know your strengths and weakness well, and have a positive view of yourself.*

*Greater **self-confidence** allows you to experience freedom from **self**-doubt and negative thoughts about yourself. Experiencing more fearlessness and less anxiety.*

*Greater **confidence** makes you more willing to take smart risks and more able to move outside your comfort zone. Having greater freedom from social anxiety.*

At the same time that I was confident and knew that I wanted a legit storefront brick-and-mortar location, I was also very cautious of all the risks and other expenses that came along with it. This meant signing a five- or ten-year lease, employees, opening accounts, and having a lot of overhead. It was a huge commitment and it made me very nervous. I had never done anything that major before and it was very intimidating.

Overhead:

Overhead *refers to the ongoing business expenses not directly attributed to creating a product or service. It is important for budgeting purposes but also for determining how much a company must charge for its products or services to make a profit.*

Regardless of the risks and my fears, I wanted a foundation for myself and was confident that if I managed it properly this store could give me that and more. I was tired of the ups and down in my life, having money then being broke and the cycle continuing. I knew that it was time for me to have a steady stream of income, build up my credit, buy a house and build a future for myself.

I was ready for the next stage in my life.

. . .

Montreal, February 2008

After a few weeks of looking around I quickly found a 2000 sq. ft. location at 1326 Rene-Emard in Pierrefonds, Quebec. It was right in front of a high school and just a few blocks away from the old location, it was perfect.

But the joy was short-lived and the anxiety hit me right away. Going from a 200 sq. ft. location to one that's 2000 sq. ft. is like driving a Honda Civic 2-door hatch back and then having to drive a fucking bus. It was overwhelming and very stressful. Initially, I had no idea what I was going to do with all this space but I eventually did.

During the negotiation with my new landlord I asked him to put up a wall in the middle of the store. I told him I needed a lot of storage space, which wasn't true. I just didn't have enough money to buy that much inventory to fill up the entire store space. I wasn't even sure if I could fill up 1000 sq. ft. of store space but I was going to try.

I signed the lease for the new location, and made plans to have a grand opening on April 4, 2008.

Fun Fact:

One year after opening, I had to break down the wall because I needed more space; two years after that, I was making an offer to buy the store next to mine because I required more space. Always believe in yourself, it will pay off.

. . .

Toronto, March 2008

With an opening date in April and the landlord doing contraction/renovations, I didn't have much to do in March so I called up my modelling agency in Toronto and told them I could spend a few weeks there working. Since I had asked them to push me internationally, they did not have much luck so I figured if I were there in their face it would help a bit. But, unfortunately, while I was there I got some horrible news.

I got a letter in the mail from the U.S. Customs and Border Protection saying that my waiver had expired and that I needed to renew it. I almost lost my mind because I had applied for a renewal. I had no idea what was going on.

With my lawyer's help, I had done an application to renew my waiver months before getting this letter so I couldn't believe this. I tried contacting them but they didn't have a customer service department for these kinds of things. I immediately called my lawyer and asked him what my options were and he said there was nothing we could do at this point. All we could do was submit a new application and hope that the first one that we sent shows up at the U.S. federal border control agency at some point.

I hung up and began to freak out.

The application process takes a month to get verified by the RCMP and then it takes up to 6-8 months to get processed and approved.

I had just signed a lease for a new store, how the heck was I going to get my inventory from New York without my waiver?

And just when I thought things couldn't get any worse, my lawyer called to tell me that he was going through my file to prepare a new application and FOUND THE ORIGINAL APPLICATION still in my file. His secretary never mailed it.

My lawyer had fucked up, and I lost it with him.

Had my lawyer not saved my ass so many times in the past, I don't know what I would have done to him. He had totally messed everything up for me. I was so totally screwed that I may have started crying.

How could this have happened to me AGAIN?

We submitted the new application, and then I moved on to try and solve my next pressing issue. I was opening the new store in a month, but I wouldn't be able to go to the US until I got my waiver, which could take up to 8 months. How was I going to get out of my lease or at least try to delay it?

. . .

I called my agency and told them I was leaving for Montreal in the morning because of an emergency and they asked me if I could come in first because they needed to talk to me.

AS IF I NEEDED ANY MORE DRAMA!!!!!

The same day I found out about my waiver was also the time that my agency got a call from a modelling agency in Cape Town, South Africa that wanted to sign me. In addition, the agency wanted me there to model during their high season, which started in two weeks, on April 15.

For a Black model, Cape Town was the place where you go to break into the international market. A Black guy with a toned body in Cape Town is like a white guy with blond hair and blue eyes in America. The opportunities in Cape Town were endless. You don't make much money but you work enough to pay for your flight, and your room and board.

The point of going there isn't about the money, it's to build your modelling book, work with bigger clients, and then come back to North America and cash in.

It was the end of March and the renovations were almost done at the store. I had no merchandise, no staff, no waiver, but I didn't give a fuck. I was way past the point of no return. It was either I break down and let fear consume me or just jump off the cliff and hope that I land without too much damage.

Fight or flight. The choice is always yours to make!

Fight or flight:

The term **'fight-or-flight'** *represents the* **choices** *that we can make.*

During this reaction, certain hormones like adrenalin and cortisol are released, speeding the heart rate, slowing digestion, shunting blood flow to major muscle groups, and changing various other autonomic nervous functions, giving the body a burst of energy and strength.

The autonomic nervous system has two components, the sympathetic nervous system and the parasympathetic nervous system. The sympathetic nervous system functions like a gas pedal in a car.

It triggers the fight-or-flight response, providing the body with a burst of energy so that it can respond to perceived dangers.

The response of the sympathetic nervous system to a stressful event, preparing the body to fight or flee (flight).

I decided to fight.

I signed the modelling contract, then tried to figure out how the heck I was going to open, hire, and manage a brand new store all the way from another continent. I had three weeks to get it all done, but I never had any fear that I wasn't going to make it.

First thing I did was to call Peaches.

. . .

Peaches
Montreal, Mid-March 2008

I told Peaches everything that happened and she was in shock. I told her that I was totally fucked and really needed her help. We agreed to meet up that night and that's when I laid out my entire plan to her.

I told her that I'd pay her whatever she was making at the YMCA and I was also very transparent and told her that she'd probably end up doing more hours than at the YMCA, but that I'd make up for it once the store was up and running smoothly.

We spoke about some other things and after a few hours we came up with a plan that we were both comfortable with, and Peaches accepted my offer that night.

Normally, I wouldn't have made a decision that quickly or asked somebody else to either, but time was of the essence. We had known each other for a few years and she had already worked at the store a few days here and there to help me out. We were comfortable with each other and knew that things would work out.

Peaches was the perfect person for the job. She didn't know anything about buying or even running a store, but she had the best customer service I've ever seen, and that's all Exclucity has ever been about anyways. The cherry on top was that Peaches already knew half of my clients from the store because so many of them played basketball at the YMCA or were members there. The store was five minutes away from the Y. It was a perfect match.

With Peaches officially on my team, I now had a full-time staff member but I still didn't have inventory.

As cool as Peaches was, I didn't feel comfortable asking her to drive to NYC alone and pick up the inventory for the store. But I had an idea about how to get her there and back safely.

I called my cousin living in New Jersey, who I was close to, and told her about the horrible situation that I was in. But I also told her that I had a solution and needed her help to execute it. My plan was to put Peaches on a bus going to New York and have my cousin meet her there with a van, pick up the inventory, and then have them drive back to Montreal together.

My cousin didn't even hesitate for a second, all she said was, "Hella ya, cuz, I'm in. What day do you want to do this?"

Family is amazing.

Our next move was to find a van big enough to fit the inventory. Don't forget we needed to fill a 1000 sq. ft. store now, not a little basement, but my cousin had a solution. She knew someone who had a church bus that seated 15 people and they were willing to rent it for cheap.

The next day I called all my suppliers in New York, and told them that I'd be sending someone else to pick up my inventory and that I needed their help. I asked them to help my cousin and Peaches pick out the styles that they knew worked best for me since I couldn't be there. This was back in 2008; I didn't have a smartphone, FaceTime or camera phone.

After a week or so of planning, everything was ready. Peaches took the Greyhound bus at midnight that would arrive at New York Penn Station at 8am. My cousin met her there and they headed straight to the suppliers.

While at home, I called them every 30 minutes to make sure everything was all right. If I couldn't physically be with them, I'd be there on the phone with them every step of the way. However, regardless of my calling and all of my planning, the day was still a mess. Lol!

They started an hour late because they couldn't find each other at the station. They couldn't find some of the suppliers and finding parking was difficult, it was hilarious. They were all over the place, running up and down, but at some point we just had to laugh at it all. It was a stressful day but it was also filled with laughs and jokes.

They didn't end up leaving NYC till after 6 p.m. and, of course, got stuck in the crazy traffic. I had to stay up to wait for them to come home because I had to meet them at the border to declare all the merchandise and pay the duties. It's not like I could have slept anyways, I was so stressed the entire time. I had my employee and my cousin driving seven hours from New York to Montreal with little to no sleep in a gigantic church bus. They were driving in the middle of the night and I was on edge.

I got to the border at 1 a.m. although I knew they wouldn't be there till 2 a.m.-3 a.m. I remember it like it was yesterday. I was there sitting in my car waiting on them and then I saw these big-ass headlights. I could tell it wasn't your standard car or truck lights. When I looked a little closer, I saw the ugliest church bus that I'd ever seen in my life and knew it was them. I couldn't be more relieved and excited to finally see them.

I literately jumped out of my car and started yelling and screaming. If you've ever been to a Jamaican party and seen someone dancing with their hands gesturing a gun salute, then you know exactly what I was doing outside of my car at the border.

I was dancing around like a big fool, completely forgetting that I was at the border where there are people with real guns. When I jumped out my car, and started yelling and screaming, spotlights came on and two SWAT vehicles came racing towards me. I quickly jumped back into my car and waited for the border guards to pull up. Luckily, I had crossed that border a million times and knew the ones that drove up to me.

Once the guards saw that I was just fooling around they told me to calm down and stay in my car. I'm glad I didn't get into any trouble.

My cousin and Peaches rolled up laughing their heads off because they saw what happened. It was really funny.

We cleared the border quickly, drove directly to the store, unpacked everything and called it a night. My cousin only stayed one day to help us out because she had to head back to New Jersey to go to work. For the next few days, Peaches and I worked around the clock to get the store set up. We called some of our friends to come help us out at the store because there is no way we could have gotten it done by ourselves. I had a lot of help from family and friends to get this store on its feet.

The night before the opening, I was at the store alone and I still had a lot to get done so I called my mother and asked her for help.

That night it was just my mom and I during the middle of the night unpacking, tagging and setting up the store. I remember saying to her, "Mom, when I was a kid, did you ever think you'd be up in the middle of the night helping me set up my first retail store?" She just looked at me, cried, and told me how proud she was of me.

That night my mom and I started a tradition, one that we haven't broken till this day. Before my mom left, she told me she wanted to buy something. I said, "Mom, what are you talking about, just take what you want." She said, "No, I want to support you, and I want to buy something at full price." She bought an $80 hoodie, and that night, technically, my mother became the first customer to buy something at that store.

Since that day, I've opened many more stores and my mom has been at each store opening. She was always the first customer and first sale at each store. Yes, even the ones outside of Montreal. I would fly her in for the day and she'd come to the store, make the first purchase and then fly back home a few hours later.

She's my good luck charm.

. . .

South Africa, April 2008

On April 4, 2008, I opened my first official brick-and-mortar location at 1326 Rene Emard in Pierrefonds, Quebec.

Till this day, I'm still amazed that I pulled it off and I did it right on schedule. Through all the ups and downs, I hadn't even open one day late. It was a great feeling and I felt very confident, BUT the job wasn't done yet.

April 15 was fast approaching and I was leaving in ten days to go to South Africa for about three months. I had a week and a half to train Peaches and get everything set up before I left. As confident as I felt, I was still very nervous about leaving because last time I left my store in someone else's hands it didn't end well. I know Peaches wasn't a 16-year-old wild kid, but still, I was leaving for three to four months and needed to make sure things stayed status quo until I got back.

I came up with the idea to buy cameras so that I could watch the store while I was away, which turned out to be one of the best moves I ever made. Till this day, every Exclucity location has cameras that I can log into from anywhere in the world. Cameras are like having a built-in 24/7 manager that you can trust 100%. Cameras will never lie to you.

Another thing that worked out well for us was the six-hour time difference. The South African time zone was perfect for me to help Peaches run the store. When I was out modelling during the day, she'd be sleeping and the store would be closed. When I got home at night the store would be open. I sat at my computer every night watching the cameras and speaking to Peaches on Skype, which she loved very much. Any questions that she had, I'd always be right there for her. I learned my lesson from the last time.

The best part of the cameras and Skype was that I was still able to talk to the clients when they came in. People would come in and I'd be there on the computer, talking and joking around with them. They all knew

I was away modelling so it was cool to touch base with them and keep the relationship going. I was looped into everything; it was amazing. It was like I never left.

After a few weeks, Peaches had everything under control at the store. She had even hired another employee so she could have a couple days off each week. While I was gone, Peaches had to go to NYC twice but she brought one of her friends with her, and everything went a lot smoother because she knew her way around.

The next three months in South Africa were amazing, and things went by really fast. I got to learn a lot about modelling, worked with a lot of big names and had a great time getting to know Cape Town. The city is like the Miami Beach equivalent for us over here, just ten times more beautiful. I also got to visit Robben Island where Nelson Mandela was imprisoned (I visited twice, it's that amazing), I went on a safari, and a bunch of other things; it was an experience of a lifetime.

The best part of the trip was that even though I was out working and exploring in the motherland, I never lost my focus on the store for even one second. I was really maturing and becoming a leader by being so much more focused on what I wanted to accomplish.

With that, I knew it was time to kick my modelling career into overdrive.

· · ·

Modelling

Montreal, July-December 2008

I got back to Montreal on July 2, 2008, but after a few months of being back home and modelling in Montreal and Toronto, I decided to go right back to South Africa for another five months to get more work and build up my modelling book some more. I still couldn't enter the US so there wasn't much I could do here.

I went back down there with no return ticket.

· · ·

South Africa (again), January-June 2009

On my second trip to South Africa, I booked several big campaigns and got to work with some major brands. I was busier than the first time I was there. I landed Men's Health, Puma, Powerade, Reebok, Daniel Hechter and Marie Claire.

I was killing it when one day I got the call that I had been waiting for a little over a year. My sister called to tell me that my waiver had arrived and I was finally allowed to enter THE UNITED STATES OF AMERICA again.

As busy as I was modelling in South Africa, the US was my dream market. I booked my ticket and flew back to Montreal that week.

· · ·

Montreal, July 2009

You're probably thinking I was excited to go back to New York for the store. Oh no my friends, the store was under control by this point. I was excited to go to the US so I could become a supermodel. I wasn't busting my ass in South Africa so I could model in Montreal or Toronto; my goal was to model in the USA!

A few days after landing in Montreal, I headed straight to Toronto to meet with my modelling agency to show all the agents my work. I was really hoping that they would love all my new work and think I was ready for the US market but, unfortunately, my agent wasn't in love with what she saw. She thought my book looked way better but she still didn't think I was ready for the big time.

I wasn't hurt by what she said to me at all. I'm someone that can take rejection really well because I don't give a fuck what people think about me anyways. These were the same people that didn't think I'd make it internationally and I did.

I walked out their office, drove back to Montreal and said to myself, "OK, fuck that, I'm going to drive to New York and look for an agency myself, I don't need them to place me. It's clearly easier to get a modelling contract if you're referred by another agency, but I wasn't about to sit around and wait for someone to think I was ready. I was born ready and I was going to get my New York contract on my own without their help.

I called Peaches on my way back to Montreal and I told her I'd be outside her house in five hours, and to get ready to go to New York. If I was going to drive all the way down to New York, I figured it would be smart to just pick up clothes for the store at the same time.

This was going to be the first time that Peaches and I would be in New York together. It was a feel-good moment of overcoming adversity but I had no time to be sentimental because I had to find an agency.

While Peaches was shopping for inventory at the suppliers, I visited the top New York City modelling agencies I could find on Google. You are supposed to make an appointment to set up meetings but I didn't care about that. I just found their addresses and walked in.

I must have visited twelve to fourteen agencies that day and regardless of my grit and determination, every single one of them said NO!

I was crushed.

Having spent the last four years modelling in Montreal and Toronto, and the past year working full-time in Cape Town, all for the chance to get signed in New York, in one day all of my dreams came crashing down on me. I felt so unmotivated and depressed that I didn't know what to do with myself. Maybe I should have made an appointment instead of just showing up at the modelling agencies, or maybe I should have listened to my agent and waited till they thought I was ready. I didn't know if I messed everything up or if it was just bad timing, or maybe I just didn't have what it takes to be in the big leagues.

I was lost and I was thinking that maybe I should just give up modelling.

. . .

A few weeks passed and then I got a call from my Toronto agency. They told me that an agency from New York City was coming to their offices the next day. The American agency was looking for some Canadian talent to sign and my agency encouraged me to come in, if I was interested.

They had no idea what I had done a few weeks before in New York. They were just calling because they knew I wanted to go to the US.

I asked them for the name of the New York agency and sure enough it was one of the agencies that turned me down just a few weeks ago. I was like, fuck that, I'm not driving down to Toronto to get rejected again. I just told my agent that I wasn't in town and that I wouldn't be able to make it.

As sure as I was that I didn't want to go to Toronto and meet the New York agency, I still couldn't sleep that night. I remember looking at the clock and it was 1 a.m. I was like, nah, fuck that, just go to bed, don't drive to Toronto; it's not worth it, don't go.

I didn't sleep one second that night and at around 4:30 a.m., I got out of bed, got in my car and headed for Toronto. I just couldn't miss the opportunity; I had to try.

The New York agency interviewed fifty models from Toronto that day but they only picked one of us to sign to their agency. And that one person was….

ME.

Being signed to a New York City modelling agency is like being at the top of the modelling food chain and it means you work all over the USA. After I got signed in New York, the ball kept rolling for me. I also got signed in Miami, Chicago, and Atlanta. Getting that New York modelling contract was probably the biggest accomplishment in my life to this point. I had really put a lot of hard work into it.

I was extremely proud of myself.

. . .

New York, August 2009

To work in the United States, I, of course, had to get a visa but my agency handled all of that for me. There are different types of visas but I was approved for an O-1 Visa.

O-1 Visa:

The O-1 non-immigrant visa is for the individual who possesses **extraordinary ability** *in the sciences, arts, education, business, or athletics, or who has a demonstrated record of extraordinary achievement in the motion picture or television industry and has been* **recognized** *nationally or* **internationally** *for those achievements.*

Basically, an O-1 Visa means exactly what I've been trying to tell you throughout this entire book. I'm extraordinary! LOLOL!!

I went from being banned from entering the United States of America in March 2008, to being approved for an O-1 non-immigrant visa in less than a year and a half. That is mind-blowing and it's for reasons like this that I wrote this book.

I'm living proof that anything is possible, even when you feel like the world is against you it's possible. You can never give up, EVER.

. . .

Becoming A Sneaker Boutique
Montreal/New York 2009

It had been five years since I bought my first Long Tee for the store and over that time Hip Hop fashion had gone through some changes, but around 2008-2009 it started making some pretty drastic changes and quickly. Even though I was away from the store in Montreal, I was living in Queens, New York, for modelling and I could see firsthand what was going on in the hood. People weren't wearing 6XL Long Tees anymore, instead they wore more fitted clothes and the style was getting a little less "street." Peaches had done a great job of noticing the shift in the threads and so did our suppliers. We were all adjusting to these broad shifts in the industry.

Our clients were also growing up and most of them had jobs now, which meant they had more money to spend and didn't shy away from high-priced items. They wanted name brands.

By 2009, most Hip Hop brands like G-Unit and Sean John had already died down, but Rocawear was still kind of hanging in there, so we opened an account to test the waters.

One of the best things I did during this time was to leave New York every weekend to work in the store in Montreal so that I could see how everything was selling, especially our selection of brands. I needed to be looped in.

I wanted to keep a solid mix of the old and the new style so that we could satisfy all of our clients as times changed. We carried a selection for the more mature clients who wanted smaller fitted clothes, but we also had the younger clients that still wanted cheap baggy no name brands from New York. You could come into the store and get a pair of no name jeans for $40 or you could also buy a pair of Rocawear jeans for $120.

Every Friday, I'd drive from Queens to Montreal but make a quick stop at our suppliers in Manhattan and pick up new inventory for the store. Peaches would do all the buying for the Rocawear and other bands that we carried in Montreal. It was such a great mix of products that there wasn't anything you couldn't find.

The store was rocking.

. . .

One day, the sales rep from Rocawear called to say they would start carrying shoes and wanted to know if we'd be interested in buying some. Right away, I said, "hell, no," because at the time I didn't want to take the risk. The sneaker business is an expensive one to get into and takes up a lot of capital. A few bad buys and that shit could bankrupt you really quick.

Capital:

*Put simply, working **capital** represents the assets you have available to turn into cash in order to pay short-term debts associated with running your **business** like purchasing inventory, equipment, and paying salaries. Cash and accounts receivable are two examples of assets that count towards a company's working **capital**.*

*It is **important** because it is a measure of a company's ability to pay off short-term expenses or debts. ... The working **capital** ratio, which divides current assets by current liabilities, indicates whether a company has adequate cash flow to cover short-term debts and expenses.*

Despite my reluctance to carry the Rocawear shoes, the distribution company was so confident that they would sell well that they offered me 120 pairs on consignment.

Consignment:

***Consignment** is a business arrangement in which a business, also referred to as a consignee, agrees to pay a seller, or consignor, for merchandise after the item sells.*

*Consignment saves the consignor **money**, because it doesn't have to buy inventory before selling it. The consignor thus avoids the overhead **costs** of managing inventory, such as storage, insurance and transportation.*

I accepted their offer and I'm very happy I did because those shoes flew off the shelves so quickly that I had to call them first thing Monday morning and ask for more.

A Rocawear mid cut boat shoe was the first sneaker that Exclucity ever sold and because of it I decided to get into the sneaker business.

. . .

Peaches would call me every day saying, "People are asking for more shoes and they won't stop asking." I was still a bit nervous about getting into the sneaker biz, but I loved the energy so much that I had to try to make it work.

I had Peaches email every major shoe brand to try and open an account but they all said no. One brand (who I won't name) said no, but thankfully, they also added the reason why they were saying no. They told us they were no longer selling to Hip Hop stores. I was shocked to hear that but it got me thinking that maybe this was the reason most of the brands said no or didn't reply to us. What I think they meant by "Hip Hop" was the old hood shops that hadn't made the transition.

Traditional Hip Hop fashion was on the way out and skate brands were on the way in, ushered by none other than Lil Wayne himself. Yup, that's right, Weezy F. Baby, "please say the baby."

Skate has always been a huge part of streetwear lifestyle, but Lil Wayne started fusing it with Hip Hop fashion. It started to get very confusing and skate became mainstream.

While Lil Wayne was ushering in skate, Jay-Z was killing jerseys by dropping one line on a track -- "I don't wear jerseys, I'm 30 plus. Give me a crisp pair of jeans...N**ga button-up."

Times were changing and brands change with the times. We had done a great job with our transitioning but it's kinda hard to convince a sales rep of that when the name of your store is "Hip Hop Exclusive," so that is why I decided to change the name of the store to Exclucity.

Not only did I change the name, but I also spent some money on the store and bought new fixtures to give it a more premium look. Once all the changes were made, I asked Peaches to email all the brands again, to send them pictures of the renovated store, and to tell them about our new direction.

It worked.

. . .

Nike

Montreal/Miami 2010

Fast-forward a year or so later and Exclucity was carrying all the major brands: Adidas, Vans, Timberland, Supra, Converse, and we were just about to get Nike. We were hot.

I had a lot on my plate at this time. I was traveling all over the US modelling so it was hard to keep up with both the store and modelling. I couldn't make all the bookings with the brands to secure product for the next season but I tried my best to be there for most.

It was just my luck that our first Nike booking was coming up and I had just gotten a modelling contract in Miami and I couldn't make it back in time.

I had trained Peaches on buying and she had done any amazing job with Rocawear and the other apparel brands. I figured I could send her alone to this Nike booking and everything would be fine. To be fair, she wasn't happy with my decision at all and didn't want to go by herself, but she went anyways. Lol!

Turns out I should have listened to her. That was a big mistake.

When we got our first shipment, I thought we got the wrong delivery, the shoes were so ugly. At the time, I didn't say anything to Peaches but I was very worried. We received a few more shipments over the next couple of weeks and it just got worse. We got about 700-800 pairs of shoes and we wouldn't have been able to even sell 50 pairs; that's how bad they were. I was so stressed that I had no idea what to do.

I decided to call my Nike rep and explain why I wasn't at the booking and begged him to help me exchange most of the order. We had been emailing and calling Nike begging them to open an account with us for over a year and now on our first order I had to call and ask to return it. That was a really risky move. He could have said no or maybe closed my account but I had no choice. There is no way I could pay for all that, and there was no way I could sell it. It would have been a straight loss.

Most companies would have never helped me out but Nike did. They took back almost the entire order and just like that they saved me. I wish I had a teachable moment here as to why Nike saved my ass but I don't. I have no idea why they did. The only thing I could think of is that maybe they just appreciated that I was honest, sincere and asked for help. I didn't try to blame it on them or Peaches or anyone else other than myself.

I knew that I was the boss and I made the final call, and with that comes good and bad decisions. I'm not perfect and I have no problems admitting when I fucked up.

. . .

Having to return that huge Nike order and book a new set of styles took a few weeks but it really developed my relationship with Nike and with my Nike rep.

Over the next two years, my Nike rep and I worked closely with each other and slowly but effectively built the Exclucity that you know today. We took our time and developed a niche business in Montreal, but neither of us could have been prepared or could have predicted what was about to come. 2012 was about to become the biggest year in sneaker history and Exclucity was perfectly positioned and aligned with Nike. Our partnership was about to take flight.

More to come in Exclucity 2 – Building a Brand

Nike x Exclucity

. . .

So, there you have it. That's my startup story.

Most startup stories are filled with fundraising, private equity investors and bank loans, but I thought it was important to show that not everyone has access to those people or opportunities. Those avenues are a privilege. Some of us have to start our business from the trunk of our car.

Never let your circumstance become your excuse.

. . .

Bonuses

My main reason for starting Exclucity was for me to grow up and have a stable foundation, buy a house, and have investments. Since I was finally making good money, it was time for me to start laying that foundation.

I bought myself a house, put a lot of money into RRSPs, and got rid of the minivan I was driving for years and treated myself to a shine black Cadillac Escalade.

After treating myself, I felt the need to do something special for Peaches as well since she had been there for me, and the store, over and over again. One day, I took her out for a performance review and told her that I wanted to do something more for her than just giving her another bonus or a raise. I asked, "If you could have one dream gift, what would it be?" She laughed and replied, "Yeah, OK, you're joking." I said, "No, I'm serious, what would it be?"

It was an inside joke between us because we both knew what her dream gift was but I just wanted her to say it. She had always dreamt of one day owning a Ranger Rover, and I knew that because she'd always talk about it.

I gave Peaches a bag with a small box in it that looked like it could fit a car key.

She literally started screaming and then she started crying.

I bought Peaches a midnight blue Range Rover with brown leather interior.

TRENT 2 | Young, Dumb & Ignorant

Young, Dumb & Ignorant

My affection for business and entrepreneurship began at 12 years old, but my ignorance as a young adult made me lose focus. I forgot who I was and what I knew I could be. During those young adult years my passion for success was overpowered by ignorance. But God had a bigger plan for me than I had for myself, and here I am as a mature adult writing a book about it.

Trust the path.

Ignorant:

*The word **"ignorant"** is an adjective that describes a person in the state of being unaware, or even cognitive dissonance and other cognitive relation, and can describe **individuals who deliberately ignore or disregard important information or facts**, or individuals who are unaware of important information or facts.*

Cognitive Dissonance:

*In the field of psychology, **cognitive dissonance** occurs when a person holds contradictory beliefs, ideas, or values, and is typically experienced as psychological stress when they participate in an action that goes against one or more of them.*

*Example: When people smoke (the behaviour) and they know that smoking causes cancer (**cognition**), they are in a state of **cognitive dissonance***

Confident

As a kid, my mother always made me feel like I was special. From the time I was five or six years old, my mom felt that she'd see my face on a billboard somewhere, or that I'd be doing something great one day because of my outgoing personality. No one else in my family has that kind of personality and my mother says she has no idea where it came from.

I don't know if my mother told me these things to build my confidence or if she really felt that way but let me tell you something, IT FUCKING WORKED! I swear to you, I always think I'm going to be amazing at every single thing I do. Even if it's something you challenge me to do that I know nothing about, I'll think I can beat you at it. It might not be right away but I'll learn it and one day soon I'll bust your ass at it. I can promise you that.

And please don't try to call me cocky, OK. I'm confident, there's a difference!

Cocky vs Confidence:

*Cocky people do have **confidence**, but it comes from a different place than true self-assurance. ... **Confident** people have a realistic picture of their own traits **and** abilities **and** trust themselves enough to respond to life authentically.*

*Many people are afraid that if they embrace their **confidence** that they will come off as **cocky**. That's just not true. **Confidence** comes from believing in yourself and having the skills to back it. ... **Cockiness**, on the other hand, is bragging or showing off without actually having the skills or know how to back it up.*

*Cockiness is not authentic. It's based in **insecurity**. It's more about making other people think you're confident as opposed to being confident.*

What I hate more than anything is when people say I only act like this because I'm rich or because I own EXCLUCITY and I think I'm the shit. Well first of all, fuck you, and secondly, fact-check me. Call anyone that's ever known me, I've been this way from the beginning. This is just how I'm built, and I don't know how to be any other way.

. . .

Trent Quality Records

Does anyone remember when CD burners first came out? If you do, do you remember if you bought one and what you did with it? I ask because I can vividly remember what I did with mine. I bought one when I was 12 years old and I started my first company.

Back in the day you could buy a CD, open and listen to it, and then return it if you didn't like it. They did that because at the time no one could burn CDs so there was no risk. Most people didn't think of buying a CD burner for hundreds of dollars when the actual CD only costs $12.99 but I looked at it differently. I thought, why not buy a CD burner and not only make CDs for myself but also make CDs for profit?

I remember thinking that my idea was genius and that this was going to turn into a big business one day and my dream of buying a Lambo would finally come true. I was12 years old, OK, don't laugh at me.

I not only bought a CD burner, but to look more professional, I went out and got labels, a printer and a rubber stamp to put labels on the CDs. I'd do some graphic work and try to match the colours, fonts and track list to the original CD and before you knew it, BOOM! I was pumping out CDs and making money.

My idea was great but I also knew that it would only be a matter of time before someone else catches onto my CD burning business and steal my idea. I figured that the timing, punctuality, consistency and quality would separate me from my future competitors.

As someone who is hypercompetitive in everything I do, I always feel that someone is going to beat me at something and there is a voice in my head that won't allow it. Coke is consistently trying to outdo Pepsi, and vice versa. It's just the way an entrepreneur needs to think.

Back in the day, new CDs always dropped on a Tuesday and you can bet that every Tuesday after school I'd be in the record store buying all the new albums. I'd rush home, burn a bunch of copies and have them ready and available for purchase the next day for all my clients. If it was a big release, I'd skip school so I could be at the music store at 10am to buy the new release, burn it and have it ready for release that day just like the stores did.

Business was great, but regardless of my entrepreneurial intellect, Trent Quality Records didn't last very long.

CD burners quickly became cheaper and were more widely available which meant more people had less reason to buy from me.

My first business was over as quickly as it began.

. . .

School

I started thinking of my next move.

At 12, I didn't know what I wanted to be in life but I knew that I wanted to be wildly successful at something. I knew I didn't want a typical nine-to-five job or to learn a trade, I wanted something else.

I wish I knew then what I know now and turned to school to help me find it, but I was young and always hated school.

What most school systems are slowly starting to realize now is that not everyone learns the same way and at the same pace. We're all built differently and we process information in different ways. Standardized testing and the grading system don't always reflect what someone has learned or understands.

Throughout high school, I had a low 60% average and thank the Lord for gym or else it would have been in the 50s. I can't honestly say I struggled in school because doing so requires that you make an effort and I made none. I just didn't listen or try because I felt like nothing applied to me.

Regardless of my failing grades, the vice-principle at my high school, Mr. Smith, had always liked me. He'd always tell my mom how smart he thought I was but he just wished I applied myself more.

I think he liked me because I was in detention all the time and the detention room was beside his office. I would make that man crack up laughing each and every day; he loved me. Come to think of it, everyone in the main office loved me. There was a teacher who refused to have me in her classroom so I spent one period each day in that office. I was there A LOT.

One day, Mr. Smith came up to me and said, "Trent, we're starting a program called Embarkations and I think you should apply." The program was built on the same curriculum as the rest of the school, it was just taught differently.

The first major change was that we didn't go to the teachers' classrooms; they'd come to us. If I remember correctly there were 20-25 students in the program and we had complete control of the classroom, it was OUR room. We had couches, benches, big desks, a full kitchen, etc. It felt more like a house than a classroom.

We decided the schedule and what we wanted to learn each day. For example, instead of seven 50-minute periods, (which means 7 different subject per day), we could do one or two subject per day. It was all up to us.

It was this Embarkations program that let me know I was going to be okay in life. I knew from then on that I was just wired differently. Put me in the proper setting and I could be very successful.

That year, I was failing and went from a low 45% average to being on the honour roll in the next semester with an over 80% average.

It was such a great feeling because so many teachers at that school hated my behaviour (justifiably so) and had given up on me, except for Mr. Smith and my mom.

Yes I was bad, spoke back, was always late and all I ever did was talk to girls and pass them notes in class. And yes, I tried to cheat on every test, and every time the teacher turned around to write on the chalkboard I would be doing some dumb shit to distract the entire class, BUT that was no reason to give up on me. Those teachers were just mean. Lol!

They also didn't like me because they thought that I started the fire in a teacher's office to get out of doing a test, but it wasn't me. I was ready for the exam and didn't burn that man's office down. How could they think such a thing of me…I was a model student lol!

. . .

Service Business

The summer after Embarkations I was riding high. I had proven what I knew all along. I was smart and just needed to be in control, as simple as that. Now it was time to find out what that meant.

With my failed CD business behind me I figured why not try the service business.

Service vs. Product business:

*At the heart of it, the main difference is that a **product business** sells physical, tangible objects, whereas a **service business** provides value through intangible skills, expertise and time. The marketing techniques and costs vary when you're selling **services versus** selling products, as well.*

In a product-based business you have to keep re-investing your money into products and there is always a risk of loss. Meanwhile, in a service-based business there are bigger upfront costs but lower risk of losses and that's what interested me.

The loss would be of your time sitting around doing nothing if you don't find clients, and me not finding clients was impossible. That's is what I do best.

. . .

My friend had already started cutting a few lawns around the neighbourhood (all within walking distance of our houses), but his dad was about to buy him a used Jeep and a trailer so he could expand his business. Since there was no way my parents would ever be able to buy me a car, I figured I'd team up with him and we'd work together.

All I had to do was buy a lawnmower and that was it, the only other expense was buying gas each week. With my upfront cost at a minimum, I was all set to go with my new enterprise and new business partner. I thought we were about to KILL IT!

I was only 15 years old at the time but I planned to wipe out all the competition in the area, professional landscapers or other kids in the area that dared to test us. Unfortunately, there were a couple of things that I didn't plan on, or had simply overlooked.

Working outside in the heat ALL DAY LONG is a pain in the ass!!!

There were a few other minor issues that I had overlooked as well. Things like customers calling to complain and having to go back and redo their lawns. Another major thing that I didn't plan on was that we'd have to provide our service regardless of the circumstance, like rain, for example. If it rained for two days, we'd have to make up for those two days when it was sunny. That sucked, and customers would call nonstop. Basically, every customer you have in the service business is your boss. You're tap dancing, smiling, and putting on a show for each one of them; I hated it.

A product-based business is sooooo much different.

If I didn't feel like making CDs, I just didn't make them. You can't call and yell at me for not making CDs. Yes, it's not great for business if

I don't have product in stock, but you don't have a contract with me so you can't make me do anything. You have way more control over your time when you're in a product-based business. In a product-based business your money works for you, in a service-based business you work for your money.

Yes, you could hire people to do the service work for you but that creates another issue. That person's work reflects on you and your brand, and if they suck you've failed because of it. The other problem is that most times if the person you hire is good they just end up leaving you to go open their own business. You're then screwed because now you have all these contracts but not enough workers to provide the service. It could be a real nightmare.

You can make a shit load of money from a service-based business but it's just not for me.

The other major lesson I learned from this lawn mowing adventure was that I HATE HAVING A PARTNER. Don't get me wrong, I'm a team player. I played football, basketball, etc., but when it comes to business, I think it's best for me to play it as an individual sport.

I think a co-owned business is better suited when people have their own strengths and departments. For example, a chef and someone who likes to manage, that's a good team. One is in the back cooking, while the other is focused on the front of house. But even then, it's hard because you have to align on everything and that's not easy. One has to be more amenable than the other; you can't have two alphas co-owning a business.

It's nice to have a partner to share the workload, the stress and the losses when times are bad. They have way more invested than an employee could ever have, but it's just not for me.

. . .

Kicked Out of School

Things started going a bit left for me in Grade 11. I lost my focus on being an entrepreneur and began thinking maybe there were some easier ways to make money.

Before I start, let me give you some context.

Growing up in my neighbourhood, I didn't have any friends to get in trouble with but that changed when Justin, one of my cousin's friend, moved from LaSalle to my neighbourhood. He started going to my high school. Although I didn't know him that well, I knew we'd get along perfectly.

LaSalle, a borough of the City of Montreal, is where I was born, but we subsequently moved during my childhood to the suburbs. They called LaSalle "Lil Texas" because of how wild it got so that should tell you about the environment.

My cousin's mom knew Justin well because she was a pre-school teacher and there wasn't a Black kid from LaSalle that she didn't know. She knew what all the kids were up to and as a result my aunt and mom were petrified of me hanging out with Justin. They knew he'd be a bad influence.

Bad influence or not, I couldn't care less, I was just happy to have some more Black people living near me. My high school had five, maybe seven Black kids in total. I grew up in a white neighbourhood and I was excited to know that Justin and his two older sisters were going to be living just a few blocks away. It wasn't like we were complete strangers because my aunt knew their family well. I met Justin and his sisters a few times back in the day when I was younger and going to LaSalle for sleepovers at my cousin's house on the weekends. They were a cool family to hang with.

Justin and I were the same age and had a similar personality. I finally found my partner in crime.

Despite my excitement at having Justin at my high school, I had to wait a little while to start hanging out with him. Although his family moved in at the beginning of the school year so that he could start school on time, Justin didn't end up doing so that year. You wanna know why?

He got arrested and was in juvenile jail.

When I found that out, I thought that was the coolest thing ever!

I had a new best friend.

. . .

Anyways, back to the story.

Grade 11 was a rough year for me, there was no more Embarkations program and I was really falling off the track. Halfway through the school year, I was kicked out because the school was sick and tired of my troublemaking. As a result, I had to finish the rest of the year at home.

The deal was that I'd go to the school on Mondays to pick up the week's homework and to drop off the previous week's assignment. That was all I was able to do as I was banned from the school on the other days.

So, if Monday was my school day, what do you think I did the rest of the week? Homework? Study? …………

HELL NO…I hung out with Justin, of course.

What a crazy year, I still don't know how I graduated. I think, technically, I only graduated from Grade 11 because Mr. Smith helped me out. If it weren't for him, I might not have gotten my high school diploma.

After graduation, I didn't try to start a business or do anything productive like I would normally do during the summer. I just wanted to hang out with Justin and his crew from LaSalle, pick up girls, drink, smoke and get into trouble.

My mother's, and aunt's fears were coming true.

. . .

Throughout the year, Justin and I had gotten really close doing stupid shit as kids. But now we were getting older and needed to start making some money. The stupid shit continued, just with more serious things. Being the entrepreneur that I was, I hated buying weed off someone when I knew I could get it so much cheaper if I bought it in a bundle. So, just like that, one day I decided to start selling weed.

I wasn't a huge dealer but it was enough to make some decent money. I had some friends who were doing some stupid things for money like robbing people of their cash. I wanted something more entrepreneurial, something that I could build, invest and multiply.

Justin was also selling weed but he got himself into a little situation and needed to make some more money quickly, the profits from weed weren't enough for him.

Justin's girl was pregnant and they both wanted to move out, find a place, and support their family. He needed some adult money.

Becoming a father at any age is stressful but more so when you're a teenager with no money. Justin had to go from being a teenage boy with no responsibilities to being a father real quick. He was embarking on a whole other level of responsibility. He used to need money for weed, drinks, partying and girls but now required money for rent, diapers, and food.

At the time, Justin felt that he had no options. He got an apartment in LaSalle with his girl but she didn't have much to offer for rent and other expenses either. Both were struggling and needed to make some money quickly.

Justin started selling crack.

I could have started selling with him but there was no need for me to do that. I understood why he felt that he had to but we were at different stages in our lives. At the time, I was still living at my parents' house and didn't know what the hell I was going to do with my life. But I knew I didn't want to sell crack, nor did I feel like I had no other options.

I was also still in CEGEP, the equivalent of a community college, at the time (in Quebec, we graduate from Grade 11 then do two years of CEGEP, and afterwards start university), but I was failing badly. I had no idea what I was in school for, I was just there to be there. I knew I liked business but didn't want to go through all that schoolwork to get a business degree.

I had my mom telling me that all I needed to do was get an education and everything would be OK in life, but I also knew that school wasn't for me. I just didn't think I could excel in a typical school environment.

Furthermore, all of my best friends were on the streets hustling and making easy money. I was so confused and had no idea what the fuck I wanted to do.

. . .

I had just failed three of my four classes in my first semester at CEGEP, which automatically puts you on probation. To get off probation, I'd have to go into a room with four heads of the school and convince them to give me another chance to come back. I was prepared to just drop out and hit the working world, but my dear mother had other plans for me. My mother begged me to attend the meeting and try to get back into the school. She even insisted on going with me so she could make sure that I actually did.

At the meeting, I told those four men that I was there because my mother begged me and that I felt it was best for me to take some time off and figure things out. They had heard this same story many times before but I also told them about my entrepreneurial ideas for the future. I told them about the small companies that I started over the years and we just ended up having a really good conversation. We spoke for about half an hour and at the end of the meeting we agreed that it was best for me not to come back to the school because I wasn't ready.

I told them how sad my mother was going to be, and that she was waiting for me outside and would burst into tears when I gave her the news. "I'll come outside with you and speak to her for you," said one of them.

"Miss, I see a lot of kids come through here each semester begging us to get back to school, but I haven't seen a lot like your son. I came out here today to tell you that you have nothing to worry about with your boy, Trent, here. He gave us his reasons why he should not come back and it's one of the best probation meetings we've ever had. You raised a good kid and he has a good head on his shoulders. I promise you, he's going to be successful in life. You don't have to worry and if he ever decides that he wants to come back, we'd love to have him," he said to my mother.

That wasn't what my mother wanted to hear. She had a huge smile on her face because of the praise he gave me but her heart was broken. She thanked him for his kind words and started crying as we left.

I felt so bad because I could understand why she was heartbroken. All she ever wanted in life was an opportunity to have a good quality education and here I was throwing away that chance. I didn't understand that then but I get it now.

Ignorant.

Fun Fact:

Every time I accomplished something big, I joked with my mom about that meeting and what the man said to her about me being successful.

In 2016, I bought my mom a brand-new Mercedes-Benz. It was her first brand-new car as all her life she had used cars. I drove it up to her house with a big red bow on it and the first thing I said to her was, "I guess that guy in CEGEP was right."

It's our little inside joke.

. . .

Fresh off of being a dropout, I did what most dropouts do.

LOOK FOR A JOB.

I knew I liked sales and doing my own thing so I looked for a sales rep position. The first one I found was selling kitchen knives. It was kind of like working for yourself so it was cool. I had to buy my own set of knives, $500 for the set, do a week of training and then I'd be on my own to sell door-to-door independently.

I did the training and then slowly started to realize that this was all a hustle; it was a pyramid scheme. They recruited people and made money off them, and so on. So basically, I was someone's hustle and I hated that.

I ended up selling three sets, all to my family, and then I quit.

I looked around at a few other places, but didn't have much luck at all. Getting hired for a job was a lot harder than I thought. Trying to find a job as a Black kid in Montreal is hard enough but not being fluent in French is career suicide. Google French laws in Quebec and you'll understand what I mean.

Not working or going to school was a recipe for disaster for a kid like me. My father always told me, "The devil finds work for idle hands." He was right because there was a Friday night when the devil found work for me for real and it changed my life forever.

. . .

Arrested

It was a cold winter night and I was in LaSalle chillin' with Justin and his crew at his apartment. He used to live in a run-down apartment building on a street that had a few crack spots, prostitutes on the corner and crackheads all around. This is nothing like living in the suburbs but for some reason I didn't mind it at all. I actually loved going there and spent almost every weekend there.

One Friday night, we left the apartment to go and get food. I was heading to the front entrance, like we normally would, when Justin said, "

Nah, we going to the back, I got a car." At first, I thought he was just joking because of two things:

1 - Justin didn't have a license.

2 - JUSTIN DIDN'T HAVE MONEY FOR A DAMN CAR.

I followed them to the back but I was a little nervous because I had no idea what was going on. Justin saw that I was feeling uneasy about the situation. As we walked to the back, he pulled me aside and said, "Just want to let you know that the car is stolen but there is nothing to worry about because the plates are clean."

There is nothing to worry about. What the fuck does that even mean. The car is stolen, but the **PLATES** are clean????

Let me explain.

Justin and his crew would steal cars and then drive around in them looking for the same make, model and colour. Once they found them, they would switch the license plates so that their stolen cars had the fresh plates, and the other cars would now have the plates of the stolen cars.

The person who gets pulled over with the stolen plate would ultimately get treated like a criminal and have to prove their innocence.

Today, as an adult I can't understand how I was Ok with that, but back then, all I could think was, "Ok cool, we're safe, the plates are clean." I thought those guys were geniuses.

We drove around that night smoking, drinking, and getting food as if nothing was wrong. It was just a stolen car packed full of young Black kids in denial, without a care in the world. However, trouble was lurking, it was inevitable.

After a few hours of joyriding, we pulled up to a red light and, of course, who pulls up right behinds up?

That's right, you guessed it, the boys in blue.

They didn't turn their lights on but we all knew what was about to go down.

Justin calmly says, "Everybody just relax, I've got a plan."

"We are right down the street from the park. When the light turns green, I'm going to turn down the street and head towards the park. When we get there, we'll all jump out the car, hop the fence and outrun the police."

I remember thinking to myself that this was a good plan. There was no way these fat-ass old cops would catch five Black kids jumping over a 12-foot fence and running through the park. I thought we could pull it off.

Boy, was I was wrong.

These cops didn't just see us at the light. They had been following us for like ten minutes and THEY HAD A PLAN OF THEIR OWN. They had been strategizing on how to catch us from before we even saw them; they were ready.

At the time, we had no idea that the cops had a trap set up for us so we were in the car super hyped, yelling, laughing and saying, "Fuck them, they can't catch us." Someone even stuck a hand out the window and gave them the finger.

This was going to be my first police chase and I couldn't be more excited.

I was READY!

Justin gets to the top of the street, sees the park then slams on the gas and takes off. The second we take off, the cops' lights come on and the chase starts.

Justin races down this little residential street at like 100km per hour and we quickly get to the park. He drives up on the sidewalk then the tires pop…BOOMMMM!!! There is smoke everywhere and we all opened the doors, jumped out and took off running for the 12-foot fence.

Once we all hopped the fence, we took off running in different directions to make it more difficult for the cops to catch us. We all knew the park like the back of our hands; this was the same park we all hung out in as kids. I knew it well because my cousin's house was right around the corner from the park. I actually thought about running there but I didn't want to take the chance of getting caught there. That would have been horrible.

Thinking that I outsmarted the cops, I ran to the far end of the park that had a Dairy Queen and a parking lot. I figured I'd go that way because it was the longest point to run to and they'd never catch me.

I was running full speed and thinking I was home free but as I turned the corner I ran smack into two police cars with four cops waiting for me.

The cops had the entire park surrounded.

When I turned the corner, I came to a dead stop and then everything went into slow motion. I felt like I was in a movie or a dream and all I could remember thinking was that I just wanted to wake up. What I actually saw were piercing bright lights and the cops yelling, "Drop your weapon, drop your weapon NOW."

I was running with my cell phone in my hand.

I thought I was going to die that night. When something like that happens you literally can't feel anything in your body, you're just completely numb and you can't even process anything. For a few seconds, your brain is frozen and your body paralyzed.

I kept hearing, "DROP YOUR WEAPON; DROP YOUR WEAPON." I snapped back to reality, dropped my phone, put my hands in the air and fell to my knees.

The cops arrested me, put me in handcuffs and placed me in the back of the squad car. There were five of us in the stolen car that night but they only caught four. We were all arrested and taken to the local police station.

I had to spend the night in jail but for some reason I wasn't bothered by it. I didn't know why but at the time I just couldn't give a fuck. I had dropped out of school, couldn't find a job and Justin's life seemed more appealing to me than any other option I had at the time. I assumed that getting arrested and going to jail was part of life so I accepted it as such.

I may have not cared about spending the night in jail, BUT I was under 18 so they had to call my parents to come and get me and that scared the shit out of me. I knew that wasn't going to go over well at all with my parents.

I hated my dad at the time so I didn't care what he thought, but I felt bad for my mom. I knew my mom would lose her mind, be extra stressed out, and be soooooo disappointed in me. I always hated making her feel any of those emotions.

My parents came to get me in the morning and it was exactly what I thought, a nightmare.

My dad was yelling, my mom was crying, and all I wanted to do was go back to Justin's apartment. I was the only one still living at home and dealing with parental drama. I felt bad for my mom but I still didn't want to go home.

That night I decided to move out of my parents' house and into my grandmother's in LaSalle. It was perfect, she lived five minutes away from Justin's apartment.

I was 17 years old, living in LaSalle, not going to school, not working and I just spent a night in jail. Things were not looking good for me but they were about to get worse.

. . .

Justin was rolling with some of Montreal's most dangerous guys, which now meant I was hanging with them too.

I'll never forget one night we were all out at a club and my sister's boyfriend (now husband), who is no stranger to the hood, saw who I rolled into the club with and he freaked out. Neither he nor my sister said anything to me that night. But my sister called me the next morning crying and begging me to come back home because she was so afraid. I was so ignorant at the time that her plea went in one ear and out the other.

While I was technically hanging with Justin's crew, I really wasn't doing anything wrong or illegal with them at the time. I was just lingering around, trying to figure out how I was gonna fit in and what I was going to do with my life. No one was pressuring me to do anything, but I was hard on myself to do something and quickly.

One of the older OG's in the crew that Justin was hustling for really took a liking to me and he would give me money on the side without anyone else in the crew knowing. This OG was the "muscle" in the crew, he was fully crazy BUT he was also one of the nicest guys I'd ever met, which was so often the case.

I remember meeting a girl one night in the club and we were in a corner talking all night long. The OG saw us talking and he could tell that I liked her but he also knew I had no money. He walked over to me and said, "Yo Trent, I'm out. Enjoy your night." He dapped me up quickly and put $200 in my hand.

That stood out to me so much, only a thoughtful person would do that. I was amazed that this guy could be so cold-hearted one minute but be the nicest guy the next. It was that OG that told me not to start selling drugs or to work for them just because I needed money. He could tell that I was conflicted, and that I was thinking about it but he told me not to. He said, "Trent, this life isn't easy, it's not what you see on TV. Do something different."

That got me thinking.

No one grows up as a kid wanting to be a murderer, drug dealer or a thief. We are all products of our own environment. If I didn't have a father that got a second job and my mother that worked nights, both trying to give me a better opportunity, where would I be?

I know I ended up hanging out in the hood regardless of my parents' efforts, but I was there because I chose to be there and because I was being ignorant. These guys were there because they had no other choice and it's all they ever knew. They didn't really want to be there.

There are a lot of amazing people in the hood that are extremely smart. They are talented and just as gifted as some of the guys that run Fortune 500 companies but they will never be given a chance to live out their true calling, and that's unfortunate. They are running a business in the streets that has the same obstacles as a legit one. They manage staff and profitability, they pivot when they face challenges, and they expand and grow their business. They are CEOs in their own right but their talents and priorities are just misguided.

Slavery, systemic racism, and oppression put our brothers and sisters at a huge disadvantage.

. . .

I had been living in LaSalle for a few months, lingering around, and having my friends always paying for me wasn't going to cut it anymore. I needed to make money of my own so I started looking at how I could make some real cash quickly.

There was a group of girls that Justin knew who were stealing stuff from stores, but I'm not talking about just stealing a pair of pants here and there. I'm talking about a huge operation of stolen goods. They were looking for a driver since their old driver was in jail.

I wouldn't only be their getaway drive. They also needed someone to go inside the stores with them to play the role of their boyfriend while they were stealing. It would be my job to distract the staff on the floor while they were stealing. I'd laugh and joke with the sales people on the floor, while the girls were stealing as much stuff as they could.

We'd literately go to every mall and stand-alone store in Montreal and when we were finished with those stores we'd go to Ottawa. We knew which stores had cameras and those that had alarm tags. We had disguises and wigs and all kinds of tricks to change things up if we wanted to repeat stores. I kept an Excel file of where we went, what we were wearing, and the date we were last there.

We had a great operation going.

For me, the best part of working with these girls was the driving. I had a reputation for my crazy driving; no one could test me. The girls and I got into a few police chases when the stores called the cops on us. But the cops never caught us once when I was driving. If you think I was crazy when I was driving my own car, you should see me drive a stolen one. I must have destroyed one car per month back in those days; it was bad.

I was just young, dumb, and ignorant.

. . .

After working with those girls for a few months, I decided to do some other things for money. I stayed in LaSalle for about 2 years and got myself into a lot more trouble, and did things I told myself I'd never do. I was arrested six times, but thank the Lord, I never did any serious jail time. I always beat the case or the charges were dropped.

The biggest crime I was ever arrested and charged with was possession of a firearm. I'm not proud of it but it's public knowledge so there is no need to hide it. Being charged with having a gun is not a joke but it was the wakeup call that I needed. Having a felony weapons charge can, unfortunately, hold you back in life and it scared the shit out of me.

Fortunately, I beat that case and was found not guilty but that was the breaking point for me.

From a young age, I knew I wanted to be someone who could walk into a bank and my name commands respect. I wanted my name and signature to be more powerful than any gun could ever be.

. . .

Struggling to Make A Change

While living in LaSalle, I'd go back home to see my parents once in a while. I'd see my dad more often than anyone else in my family because he'd come for lunch at my grandmother's house from time to time. He wouldn't say much to me and mostly left me alone to do my thing. He would say, "You're over 18 years old now, you're an adult, you can make your own decisions."

My father was playing it very smart. He knew that he had given me all the tools necessary to make the right choices in life, but while playing it cool on the surface, he was also putting together a brilliant little plan to get me to move back home and I didn't even realize it.

My father called my aunt, who lived in Los Angeles, and asked her to call me and invite me to spend the summer in L.A. I loved hanging out in LaSalle with my boys but who the fuck would turn down living in L.A for the summer.

My aunt and her six sons lived ten minutes away from Venice Beach and they owned the only reggae club in Santa Monica. The best part of the club was that on Tuesday nights it turned into a strip club. There was nothing to think about here, I said yes right away and I left the following week.

That summer in L.A was probably the best summer I've ever had in my entire life. Maybe one day I'll write a book about that summer, it was that crazy. When I got back to Montreal at the end of the summer, my dad had another trick up his sleeve that would prevent me from going back to live in LaSalle permanently.

He renovated the room I was staying in at my grandmother's house and her sister was now staying there. All of a sudden there were no more bedrooms for me and I had no other place to stay in LaSalle. I had spent all my money in L.A on weed, booze and strippers so I was broke. Guess that meant I'd have to move back home.

But at the time I won't lie, I didn't mind it that much. It was a nice break to be back home and have a home-cooked meal every day, and be in a nice house with a backyard. It was relaxing and calm, just what I needed.

My father knew exactly what he was doing by getting me out of LaSalle. He used to live there so he knew the kind of place it was and what could happen if I stayed there any longer.

His timing was perfect.

. . .

While I was away that summer, the cops raided an apartment from which the guys sold drugs and all of my friends were arrested. Some spent serious time in jail, others a few months and some got off with probation. If I was still in Montreal at the time, there was a good chance that I would have been there hanging out with them. There is no telling what the cops would have tried to charge me with.

My dad saved me big time. I just wished my friends had someone in their lives that could have rescued them also because things were getting worse in LaSalle.

One night, not too long after I got back from L.A., there was a house party happening in LaSalle. One of my friends invited me to go with him but I was still recovering from my trip to L.A. so I said no and stayed home.

My friend went to the party with some other friends and was hanging out, drinking and smoking like we usually do, but this didn't end up being a typical night.

There was a group of people in the driveway smoking and my friend was mingling and talking with them. All of a sudden he heard a loud BOOMMMM. He then felt something wet, like someone had thrown a drink in his face.

But that's not what happened....

Someone had walked up behind the guy he was talking to and shot him point blank in the back of his head. It was blood that was all over my friend's face, not a drink.

When I heard the story that was it for me. I decided right there and then that I would never move back to LaSalle. It was time for me to make a change.

. . .

Moving Back Home

I decided to take over the room in my parents' basement so that it would feel like I was living on my 'own-ish.' My parents would have allowed me to have the entire basement, if I wanted it, because they were happy to have me back at home.

For a few months, I didn't do much except stay in my room and watch TV and movies all day long. But knowing that I needed to get a job to keep myself busy or I'd just end up back in LaSalle, I eventually wrote my resume and started looking for a job.

My dad had called my step-grandfather who worked at Merck Frosst, a pharmaceutical company, and asked him if there were any job openings. At the time, I didn't know about their conversation. He told me that he heard Merck was looking for people to work in the production department and that I should apply. My dad and I may have had our differences but he always looked out for me.

When my dad told me about the salary and overtime opportunities, I was very excited. The production department had a 40-hour workweek but they did it over a four-day workweek, from 7:30 a.m. - 5:30 p.m. This meant that if there was work on a Friday it would be overtime hours, which happened most Fridays, and sometimes there was overtime on Saturdays too.

Hourly work never interested me because typically there isn't much money in it, but with that much overtime I knew I could make some good money. I applied, got an interview and was hired within a few weeks.

I was hired to work in the packaging department at an entry-level position, which was basically hell. I was on an assembly line where I packed bottles of medication into boxes. Sometimes, I'd have to watch machines to make sure they were closing bottles properly. That was the worst thing ever, I was bored but I knew I was on a good path. I was working, paying taxes and building up my **credit**!

Contrary to popular belief, cash is NOT king, credit is, and I'm happy I realized that from a young age. Being aware of that led me to make a plan for myself for the next two years. I stayed home every night, worked as much overtime as possible and put myself on a budget.

My goal was to buy a property within the next two years and to get into real estate.

. . .

My plan was going perfectly and I had an opportunity to fast track it. There was a position opening up in the production department for an assistant production coordinator and I really wanted to get out of the packaging area. The position was being a janitor and a gofer for the tablet department.

The best part was that it paid more than I was making and there were more overtime hours, which meant more money for me. Even better, I would also have a greater chance of getting a permanent position, which was something I really wanted because I was still on a temporary quarterly contract.

I applied for the position and got hired. Yes, I was happy for the pay increase but I was also glad to be on my feet, as opposed to just be sitting on my ass all day on a chair in the packaging department watching machines and packing boxes.

I was the janitor and gofer/assistant of all three sections of the tablet department: tableting, coating, and printing. I had to start work everyday before each section got in, and I finished after they left. I had to set up their rooms, make sure they had everything they needed, and then at the end of the day clean everything up. I had to mop the entire department, take out the garbage and do all the other shitty things that no one else wanted to do.

It may sound like I hated the job, but honestly I didn't mind it at all. I was just happy for the money and stability. It was the balance that I needed.

. . .

After a year and a half of working my ass off at Merck Frosst and saving money, I finally had enough money for a 5% down payment on a house. My credit was good, so getting a mortgage wasn't that hard. The bank questioned why a 20-year-old kid was applying for a mortgage and gave me a bit of a hard time because of my age, but I had everything that was required so they had to approve my application.

I was nervous about taking on such a huge responsibility, but I knew that most successful entrepreneurs had real estate in their portfolios when they were young so I knew that I was on a good path.

I also knew that owning property was one of the best assets to invest in because it's an immovable property and you can take out loans against it once there is enough equity.

Equity in your home:

Equity *is the difference between what you owe on your mortgage and what your home is currently worth. If you owe $150,000 on your mortgage loan and your home is worth $200,000,* ***you have $50,000 of equity in your home***

I bought, signed and moved into my first home two weeks before my 21st birthday and never had a co-signer or anyone lend me a penny for that house. That is something that I'm still proud of till this day.

The move out of LaSalle was good for me. I was on the right path but I wasn't in the clear yet.

. . .

I was a new homeowner but there was a problem brewing at work that I couldn't ignore.

Before me, the eight white guys that were in my role at work all got permanent positions within six to eight months. I had been working in this position for over a year and no such offer was made to me. All of my reviews were good so there was no excuse to not hire me permanently. Without a permanent position I had no protection, vacation or any sick days. I was a homeowner but I had no job security.

When I asked why I hadn't gotten a permanent position yet, all they kept saying to me was that there was nothing available, which was total bullshit. There were people leaving and retiring but instead of promoting me to replace them, they just gave their tasks to someone else in the department.

I kept asking what was going on and heard the same old bullshit, just be patient.

One day I got fed up and went to human resources and told them that I felt I wasn't being hired in a permanent position because I was Black. If I remember correctly, there were about 1500 employees at that location but only 20 were Black and very few had permanent positions.

I tried to get some of the other Black workers to file a complaint with me, but they didn't want to draw any attention to themselves and possibly lose their jobs. However, I refused to keep my mouth shut about this and one day my manager called me into his office to talk about it. Prior to this meeting, this manager was one of my favourite bosses. He was always so cool with me but that was about to change.

He told me that he had heard about the claim that I made with HR and was disappointed that I considered it a racial issue. Instead of this asshole saying something like, "Hey, sorry you feel that way. I'm here to support you, etc.," he went into defense mode saying that my claims were not true. He then said something that made me never want to work for another company ever again.

"We know you just bought a house and that you live alone. If you lose your job here, you'll lose your house and I don't think you want that," he said.

This little fucking asshole really went there.

I was on a three-month renewable contract. He knew all he had to do was not renew it and I'd have no leg to stand on. The government and major corporations are all a fucking set-up to keep you down, use you up, spit you out, and then bury you.

Think about it.

The government gives huge tax breaks and loans to these major corporations because they are the hamster wheels that the government needs to keep you running fast to nowhere on.

Why do you think the government gives you money back when you invest in RRSPs? They do that so they can keep you invested in them. The only time you can take money out of your RRSPs without getting penalized is when you're buying a house for the first time. Why do they do that? To encourage you to buy a house, stay in this country, work and PAY TAXES TO THEM and then die. Their goal is to keep you in a rat race because that's when they make the most money off of you. Any time the government does anything for you, it's really for them.

You're having a baby, GREAT! The government loves that too. They'll give you a cheque for that baby and some tax breaks. Why? They are making an investment. That little human is going to grow up, get a job, pay taxes, buy a house and give the government 100 times more money than the government ever gave them. It's a vicious cycle and that's the same bullshit Merck Frosst was trying to do to me, and I wasn't having it at all.

You're not going to back me into a corner and take advantage of me. NEVER!!! I'd rather be homeless living in a box.

I knew my contract at Merck wasn't going to get renewed because of my complaint. But I wasn't worried because this was my first and only corporate job. I was used to hustling and making money on my own. I didn't need them then, and I certainly don't need them now.

. . .

I had bought my house in July and I lost my job four months later in November, but I couldn't care less. I was happy with my decision of not keeping my mouth shut. I left Merck Frosst with my pride and dignity intact, that's all that mattered to me.

As human beings we think that we like money but what we don't realize is that what we really like are the things that money can buy us. I try to never get the two confused. I know the difference between what I want and **what I need.**

Money can't buy me peace of mind.

After losing my job, as with anything major that happens in life, I got very nervous and scared about what the future may hold. I was stressed about what I was going to do next. One of the key things that I always try to keep in mind is that whatever you lose you can always get back. If you misplace your keys, are they lost or are they just in a place where you can't find them? It's up to you if you want to put in the effort into finding them.

Through all the crap that I had to deal with at Merck Frosst, I never really feared losing my house. I always knew that even if I lost it, I'd get it back one day and I'd buy an even bigger house – I just had to figure out how to do that.

Today, as a successful businessman, not only am I a homeowner again but one of the houses I own has six bathrooms in it. I take a shit in a different bathroom every day of the week except for Sunday. I hope someone gives this book to my old manager at Merck Frosst and he reads this part. I included this paragraph just for him.

#asshole

. . .

Gambling

One day a friend asked if I wanted to get in a football bet with him. It was my first time ever gambling; I didn't even buy lotto tickets. I put in $60 on a 5-game parlay and I won $1,500 -- not bad for a first-timer. Keeping this in the back of my mind, I thought it would be a great idea to turn gambling into a full-time business and make some money.

At this point, I was 21 years old and although I was on a better path, I was still making dumb decisions. Since I had no job, I came up with the brilliant idea to start gambling so that I wouldn't lose my house.

Remember my friend Matt, the guy I used to do the lawn mowing business with? His father used to gamble every weekend and if you ever need help with any underground shit in Montreal, Matt's dad could help you and you'd be protected. He hooked me up with the right people to place my bets.

With Matt's dad's guidance, I stopped with the parlay bets and started betting one for one, straight up. You bet a $100 and you win a $100.

I started out betting with small amounts of money, but then in true Trent fashion I had to start going overboard with it. When I won $100, it didn't feel like I gained $100, instead it felt like I lost $900. I regretted not betting $1000. That's how gambling gets you addicted, that's how it sucks you in. If you lose, you continue to play hoping you'll get your money back. If you win, you want to play more hoping to win more, but there is always a loss lurking around the corner. Gambling is super addictive and when things go bad they go bad quickly.

Matt's dad used to bet on everything: NFL, CLF, college, high school, etc. If they had a football team, he'd bet on them. He loved betting on football. We were pretty close; he was a cool kind of dad, more like a big brother than a dad. He was single, always drove nice cars, partied all the time, and he always had money.

Matt's dad was Italian but he told people that he slept with a Black woman and I was his son. He was a real joker. Sadly, and it breaks my heart every time I think about it, he was murdered when I was 24 years old. He never got to see what I made of myself. I know he'd be proud me.

#rip

. . .

When I started gambling, I kept it simple. One for one, and I'd bet over and under and never the spread. To me, at that time it was the smartest bet. (There are no smart bets in gambling, that's how gambling gets you. It makes you feel like you've figured it all out.) In my head it was simple, why bet on how much a team is going to win by, to me that's too much risk. Regardless of who's better or worse, or who wins or loses, both teams have to score so the over and under bet was the smarter move to me. The only outside factor that could mess things up was the weather; but I had a plan for that. I only bet on teams that played in a dome, I thought I was so smart.

I was making money and starting to feel very confident about gambling. I started out betting $100 per game, then quickly moved up to betting $1000-$2000 on some games. I'd lose big some weekends but I'd also win big sometimes too.

Unfortunately, with these wins and loses I was only making enough money to scrape by from betting on football so I decided to take it up a notch. I started going to the casino. I'd pick up my football winning from my bookie Monday evening and then head straight to the Montreal casino to play Blackjack.

I started going to the casino 3-4 days a week; I turned gambling into my nine-to-five job.

If you ask any gambler, they will tell you that gambling is based on skill, not luck. That's the reason so many people end up broke. I was great at predicting football scores but I was mediocre at Blackjack. You keep telling yourself you're going to figure it out but that's just bullshit. It becomes your excuse to keep going back, cognitive dissonance.

When I first started playing Blackjack I was horrible. I didn't know the signs, when to hit, to stay or to double down, I knew nothing. I'd hit on 14 when the dealer was showing a 3, just in hopes that I'd get to 21. People would get up from the table because when you hit and you're not supposed to, the real gamblers will want to kill you for messing up the deck. They felt that the card you just took was meant for the dealer to bust and you made them lose the hand.

Anyways, there's an entire science and way to playing Blackjack, and who do you think taught me how to play it…Matt's dad, of course.

. . .

I gambled "professionally" for about a year. The first six months started out really well, I was paying my mortgage and had a car but that didn't last long.

Things started going downhill for me quickly. I had a line of credit and a few credit cards that I used if I lost big, and there wasn't much room left on them.

Stupidly, I got myself into a deep hole that I couldn't get out of. I was running out of money, maxed out my credit and I couldn't keep up with my payments.

I stopped going to the casino and betting on football and I turned to the only person that I knew could help me, Matt's dad.

. . .

White Collar Crime

If Justin was the one to introduce me to the hood, Matt's dad was the one who introduced me to white-collar crime.

White-Collar Crime:

White-collar crime refers to financially motivated, nonviolent crime committed by businesses and government professionals. It was first defined by the sociologist Edwin Sutherland in 1939 as "a crime committed by a person of respectability and high social status in the course of their occupation."

Since dropping out of school, I had tried a few different ways to make money but nothing really worked well. I tried in the hood but my friends were going to jail and people getting killed so I knew I didn't want to go back to that. I lost the only corporate job I ever had due to racist assholes so I knew the corporate world wasn't for me. Then I tried gambling and that was a disaster.

I was lost.

When Matt's dad started schooling me on some of the ways he was making money, it was like music to my ears. At that time, white-collar crime sounded like it was the best thing in the world. It didn't involve guns, drugs, or violence and was solely focused on financial gain.

Where do I sign up? Who do I submit my application to?

I was in!

. . .

Bankruptcy.

For those of you who don't know the details of bankruptcy, I'll give you a quick explanation. When you file for bankruptcy, you're basically released from every contract you've ever signed. There are a few things that you can't get released from, but for the most part it's everything.

Here's an example:

If you have a mortgage, car loan, line of credit, credit cards, store card or any sort of loan or lease, when you file for bankruptcy you are released from all those obligations and you don't have to pay them anymore. You will be debt-free.

That's the good part. Here's the bad part.

You lose everything you own. You'll lose your house, car, savings and anything thing else of value, anything that a trustee can take and sell off to pay your creditors. They can't take your clothes or anything that you need to live but everything else is gone.

The other downside is that you're basically frozen for nine months. You can't sign for anything or have anything in your name and if you're working they will take money from your paycheque.

It doesn't end there.

Bankruptcy stays on your credit report for seven years, and it's a bitch to get credit within those seven years. If you want any form of credit you're going to need a strong co-signer and be prepared to pay very high interest rates.

Lastly, bankruptcy is never fully removed from your name. It's attached to you for life. It doesn't show on your credit report after seven years but banks can search and find it.

The bad parts of bankruptcy are meant to scare people away from doing it. But when you're young, dumb and ignorant it doesn't frighten you one bit. I also wasn't scared because I had Matt's dad showing me some tricks.

I had a mortgage, a maxed-out line of credit, and a bunch of maxed-out credit cards, and I didn't have to pay any of it back.

After filing for bankruptcy, I quickly moved onto the other hustle that Matt's dad taught me.

Insurance fraud.

. . .

Insurance fraud:

Insurance fraud is any act committed to defraud an insurance process. It occurs when a claimant attempts to obtain some benefit or advantage they are not entitled to, or when an insurer knowingly denies some benefit that is due.

I started making insurance claims every couple of months.

All of a sudden my car got stolen, my girlfriend's car got stolen, my house flooded; things like that. One of the biggest claims I ever made was that my house got robbed, but this claim didn't go as smoothly as the others and led to an investigation.

The police and insurance company began investigating whether the break-in at my house was staged, (which is a felony) and they also looked further into my insurance claim to find out if it was fraudulent.

My claim was lavish, but that's what happens when you keep getting away with things, you keep coming back for more because you think you're untouchable and won't get caught. I claimed that I had lost a lot of jewelry, cash, audio equipment, clothes, cell phones, ten TVs and six computers.

This time I had gone too far.

The police brought me in for questioning but I played dumb and went along with the investigation hoping that they wouldn't find anything and close the case.

After the interrogation, I started feeling paranoid. I had hidden my TVs, computers, and a few other things in Matt's dad's garage before I filed the claim, but I started feeling that I should move them, so I did. I moved my things from Matt's dad's garage, split them up and hid them in the houses of friends.

Fast-forward a couple of months. I had to move out of the house I was living in, because the bank was repossessing it, to another house that I had just rented. On the day of the move, I decided to pick up my TVs and computers from my friends' houses to put them in mine. The investigation was ongoing but it had been so long that I figured they weren't going to do anything at this point and it would eventually be closed.

BIG MISTAKE!!

A few days after I moved into my new place, I heard a knock on my door. I looked out my bedroom window and saw three cars outside my house. There were two unmarked cars and one regular cop car. I contemplated running out the back door but I didn't. They had all my info anyway and would have eventually found me.

I didn't open the door right away because I didn't know what to do. I thought they would eventually break the door down but they didn't. They just continued knocking and rang the doorbell a few more times.

They definitely weren't like the cops from LaSalle who would have busted down the door and not even knocked. I think that's what relaxed me and helped me to make the decision to open the door and deal with my fate.

When I opened the door, the cops gave me a piece of paper and said, "This is a search warrant, we have the right to search your home." I let them in and, of course, I knew what they were looking for.

There were six cops in my house; it was like a small task force. I asked, "Is all this necessary, do you really need six cops here?" They replied, "YES, just sit down and shut up."

As the cops began searching my house, they were talking among themselves and I picked up on something. They weren't there to try to find a TV or two, instead they were there trying to find 100 TVs and a bunch of other things.

The police thought I had a huge insurance fraud operation going on and they were coming to bust it. That's why there were six officers in my house. They didn't think I was just some stupid young adult repeatedly making false insurance claims, they thought I was running a bigger operation than it really was.

They took pictures of the few things that they found but they were really pissed off that they didn't find much more. They asked me several questions, including where was I hiding the other stuff but I didn't say a word to them.

The cops tried to scare me by telling me that they had more search warrants for other locations, but that didn't work. If they had other search warrants, the last thing they'd do is tell me about it. I wasn't buying it for a second.

I wasn't sure if the few things that they found in my house were enough to arrest me so I sat there and waited as they called their sergeant for approval. I think the judge that serves a warrant has to approve an arrest if the cops don't find exactly what they thought they'd find.

After an hour or so of searching and waiting, I heard one of the cops in the kitchen say, "Yes, it's approved." I knew that it was over.

I was arrested, charged, and taken to jail.

. . .

The cops didn't have enough evidence to find me guilty on all the charges they wanted to but they had enough for two lesser charges.

At first, I pleaded not guilty and my lawyer tried to get the case thrown out. He tried everything he could but there was no luck. The cops didn't make any mistakes. It was a clear-cut case and there was no way I could have won. On the day of the trial, I had to change my plea from not guilty to guilty so that the judge would grant me leniency.

Even though, technically, I lost the case, I still won because the cops were trying to charge me with other things. They wanted me to do jail time. I pleaded guilty to a lesser charge of insurance fraud over $5000 and obstruction of justice. I had to pay a fine and do community service but no jail time.

. . .

Taking Accountability

I had been kicked out of school, arrested, and now I had a record.

I was a defiant kid that didn't listen to my parents and had no respect for the law. I thought I could do whatever I wanted to do and get away with it.

It was time for accountability.

Accountability:

*Accountability eliminates the time and effort you spend on **distracting activities and other unproductive behaviour**. When you take accountability for your actions, you're effectively learning how to value your time.*

*Webster's Dictionary defines "accountability" as "the quality or state of being accountable; an obligation or **willingness to accept responsibility for one's actions**."*

*Accountability **doesn't mean punishment**.*

Accountability is a willingness to accept responsibility for our own actions.

. . .

When you're finally ready to be held accountable for your actions, then and only then, is when you can start making effective and substantial change in your life.

These were the seeds that grew into EXCLUCITY.

EXCLUCITY 2 | Building a Brand

Building a Brand

Building a brand is like raising a child. You give birth to it, then you spend sleepless nights protecting, guiding, and nurturing it. When it's older and finally goes out into the world you spend your days nervously hoping that you raised your brand right, and that you gave it all the tools needed to survive in this fast-paced, sometimes cruel world.

Like parents watching their children graduate, go off to university, get married and start a family of their own, if you raise your brand effectively and with love, you too can sit back and watch the fruits of your labour prosper.

A Brand:

Branding is a way of identifying your business. It is how your customers recognise and experience your business. A strong brand is more than just a logo — it's reflected in everything from your customer service style, staff uniforms, business cards and premises to your marketing materials and advertising.

Your brand is the sum of people's perception of your products, vision, and content. Everything you do influences the perception that others have of your brand. It's one of the most important parts of entrepreneurship. It can make or break you.

Anyone can open a company, but only a few can build a brand.

Nike All Star Galaxy Pack

In Exclucity 1 – Building a Startup, I covered how I went from the trunk of my car to having a retail store that carries all the major sneaker brands. All of that was just the foundation, but it wouldn't be until 2012 that I really started building a true brand. Everything started with the Nike All Start Galaxy Pack.

Here's how it all happened.

Nike's secret weapon is the people they hire. I've been blessed to have the best of the best work on my account but there is one Nike employee that stands out above all the rest -- Nick Nestor.

The 'N' in Exclucity, stands for Nick. (That was just a joke, but you get what I'm trying to say.) Nick and I are both very similar and get along really well. He's Black, bold, outspoken, and incredibly ambitious.

In 2010, Nick was working in the Nike Toronto Canadian head office as a customer service rep but he was very eager to move up the proverbial ladder and become a sales rep.

Regardless of his eagerness, Nick also knew that he'd have no chance of getting the sales rep position in the Toronto office in the near future. However, there was a sales rep position opening up in Montreal so he quickly applied, got it and devised a plan. Nick wanted to aggressively grow the Montreal market and make a name for himself so that he would be noticed and eventually move back to Toronto for a bigger position. He was dialed in and super focused on what he wanted to do.

Prior to meeting me, Nick had already approached a few other Montreal stores that were bigger than mine. He asked them if they were interested in growing their Nike business by buying a broader assortment of Nike product. Every store he approached was hesitant and said no.

I know this sounds crazy to you right now but don't forget this is late 2010. Nike had just come out of a little slump and many of the stores he was asking to buy more products were probably not making a lot of money with Nike at the time, so they wouldn't be eager to accept his offer.

Outside of Jordan (that wasn't as super hyped up as they are today), there wasn't much reason for stores to take Nick up on his offer. On top of that, the category that Nike and Nick were trying to grow the most was basketball. At that time, no one was wearing on-court basketball shoes as fashion.

The LeBron 8 was out at the time and it was a popular shoe, but it wasn't until the LeBron 8 "South Beach" that LeBron's sneaker became really popular and mainstream.

Unfortunately, as a buyer you can't just cherry-pick the hot stuff and think that Nike is going to let you slide with that; that's not how things work. This is a business and when you buy into a category you buy into it all the way. You've got to take the good with the bad.

For example, per season Nike might release six to seven LeBron colours of the same model. You're lucky if two or three of them are a hit and sell out, but then you're stuck with four other colours that don't sell. That's the scary part about supporting a category, especially a category like Nike Basketball. Nike has a lot of signature athletes: Kobe, LeBron, KD, and more, six models per season. If you do the math, that's a lot of fucking shoes.

Regardless of the huge undertaking, I really liked Nick and I trusted him. He said he'd help me out if I really got jammed up, but he was confident we could build an order that would have good sell-through and we'd both be happy with it, so I did it.

I had just started getting into the footwear business, so I was more open to the risk. It worked out to be a very profitable decision.

. . .

Nick and I had been doing so well with our broader assortment of product that Nike took notice of us. We were invited to their Retail Summit in Las Vegas, which is held twice a year for all their top accounts and reps.

This is where Nike shows their top accounts all the new products that are coming down the pipeline. You also got to meet and talk with the big directors and vice presidents that worked at Nike World Headquarters in Beaverton, Oregon.

Relationships are key to building any great business; those Vegas trips were a game changer for me.

At the Nike City Specialty Retailer Summit in August 2011, I got to meet a legend at Nike, Jim Wood, an executive, and that's when things changed for Exclucity. Jim had been working for Nike since the early 80s. He was one of the original Nike employees and he was Nick's boss' boss.

At one point during the summit, Jim and I were talking and joking around about a few random things but then we got to the topic of Nike and how the brand was performing at the store.

He asked me how things were going and if Nick was doing a good job. More importantly, he wanted to know how our basketball assortment was looking and if Exclucity had gone deeper into the Nike basketball selections. "Yes, Nick is doing a great job, and yes, we're heavily invested in basketball. But I do have a few issues that I think you can help me fix," I replied.

I told Jim that Nike Canada wasn't doing a good enough job of bringing in all the same products that the U.S offers. For example, we didn't have Foamposites, and I thought that was hurting the Canadian sneaker market.

Foams (nickname for Foamposites) had always been a staple in the sneaker world, but it was more of an underground silhouette that was starting to cross over into the mainstream and I felt that we needed them in Canada.

Jim agreed with me but he said he was told by a major basketball store in Canada that Canadians wouldn't buy a $300 basketball shoe. I'm not going to name the store but they have stores all over the world. I like to call them "The Uniform Boys."

(More on "The Uniform Boys" later and why I don't like them. Lol!)

One of the problems with bringing in a style like the Foams into the country is that Nike has minimums. If a major account, (for example "The Uniform Boys"), doesn't like a shoe, it probably won't make it into the country because it won't hit Nike's minimum production requirements. The executives that run these major retail accounts generally care more about the numbers than about the culture. They aren't focused on what the sneaker community needs or more importantly deserves, so they are less likely to gamble on a shoe.

That's why Exclucity had such a major impact on the Canadian sneaker game when I started expanding. I ordered in such large amounts that I could evoke change in the marketplace. I could now bring in the shoes that I wanted and the shoes that I liked. I could hit my own minimums without needing the other major retail accounts to like the shoe.

As a result, more styles, and colours were able to come to Canada, giving the Canadian sneaker community a broader, more diverse assortment of sneakers.

In our channel, I was also able to evoke change in women's footwear as well, which was basically non-existent in Canadian sneaker boutiques before Exclucity. "Lead with Her" was a slogan that Nike pushed and it was one that Exclucity adopted and took very seriously. Every Exclucity location had a wide assortment of women's footwear in full view as soon as you walked in the door. This is something you'd be hard-pressed to find in any other sneaker boutique, even outside of Canada.

. . .

Anyways, let me pick up this mic and continue telling you about the conversation I had with Jim about Foamposites. Lol!!

Jim said, "Okay Trent, if you think foams can sell in Canada, I'll make sure to get some up there so you can test it out for us." He also agreed to try and have Canada and the U.S. more aligned so that when our Canadian customers saw something on a sneaker blog, they could come to stores like Exclucity to buy it.

The funny thing is that at the time Jim and I were having this conversation neither of us knew what was about to happen in February 2012 for the NBA's All Star weekend. No one knew, but it would change Nike, and the entire sneaker game FOREVER.

. . .

Nike released the Pine Green Foams in late 2011 and the Red Foams were getting ready to drop in February 2012 for Valentine's Day. I called up Nick and asked him why we hadn't gotten either of the releases and he said, "Just chill, I got you. You'll find out which Foams you're going to get when we go to Vegas in February. Trust me you're going to be happy."

There had been rumours that the highly anticipated 2012 Nike All Star Pack was going to have a foamposite in it but Nike did not confirm those rumours, so I didn't think it was true. Having a Foamposite in the All Star Pack would be monumental, but since I didn't know if the rumours were true, I just kept bothering Nick for Red Foams. At the time, I didn't care which Foams we got; I just wanted them.

A few weeks would pass and Nike eventually confirmed the rumours. Nike released official pics of the 2012 Nike All Star "Galaxy" Pack, which consisted of the LeBron IV, Kobe VII, KD IV along with the Galaxy Foamposite. There were some other shoes in the pack as well, but those were the top 4 of the pack.

Once the pics were released, the hype started to build and it built quickly.

Here is a write-up from Sneaker News:

"LeBron James, Kevin Durant, and Kobe Bryant are without question three of the most powerful forces in the NBA, traveling to unforeseen heights that few others have ever reached. A numerous collection of MVP awards, All-Star accolades, post-season successes, and international presence have placed a cosmic spotlight on these three mega-stars, and to celebrate their 2012 NBA All-Star Game selections is a special 'galaxy' theme inspired by space exploration and the supernova.

The Nike Zoom Kobe VII, Nike Zoom KD IV, and Nike LeBron 9 all feature the inter-galactic imagery with gleaming glow-in-the-dark outsoles and unique mission patches adorning each distinct shoe. The Nike Basketball 2012 All-Star Collection will become available on February 25th on the eve of the All-Star Weekend's main event at select Nike Basketball retailers."

The rumours around the pack were that the distribution was going to be super extra limited. At this point, I didn't know if the pack was even going to be available in Canada, much less if we'd be getting them, but that's what Nick's surprise was.

In Vegas, Nick and Jim surprised me and told me that because I had bought deeper into the basketball category and I was doing so well with it, Exclucity was going to be getting the complete 2012 Nike Basketball All Star Pack, including the Foamposites.

This was going to be LEGENDARY.

I literately started jumping up and down right there in the middle of the summit. But that's because I had no idea that the next few weeks were going to be the craziest and most stressful of my life thus far.

My Nike All Star Pack only got delivered a couple of days before the release. And the most coveted shoe in the entire pack, the Foamposite, only got delivered a few hours before the release. There were hundreds of people lined up outside and police surrounding my store. While all of this was happening the Midnight News was there capturing it all on camera.

Sit back and relax, this might be the best story in this entire book.

. . .

The Launch

When I got back to Montreal from Vegas, I gathered my team and told them that we'd be getting the entire pack and that I wanted to do something really special around it so that we could stand out.

Since the theme of the pack was "Galaxy," I wanted to transform and decorate the store in a space theme. We got a bunch of space decorations, planets, streamers and we rented an astronaut costume. Prior to us doing this space-themed activation, most local sneaker boutiques didn't do activations on their own. Actually, even now, most don't do it. Activations are typically something that the brands do and pay for.

I knew this All-Star Pack was going to bring us A LOT of attention, so I was willing to invest in myself and create my own activation. It would turn out to be one of the best investments that I ever made, especially since it wasn't that expensive anyways.

Everything was set. All I needed now were the shoes to arrive. Typically, we get our deliveries anywhere from 14 to 7 days before the release date, but it all depends on the Nike Distribution Centre. Nick told me that because this was such a unique release, we would only be getting our shipment 7 to 5 days before the release. He said it would make it there on time and that there was nothing to worry about.

. . .

Ten days before the release, there was an article on a sneaker site reporting that people in New York City had already started lining up outside of sneaker boutiques waiting for the Foamposite Galaxies. The lining up part wasn't the thing that was out of the norm; it was the timing of it that was shocking. People had lined up for Jordans and SBs before this, but not 10 days in advance. That is not common.

When that article got posted, more people started to line up at other sneaker boutiques across the US. The mayhem was starting. We got a lot of calls about the pack because we had already announced we'd be releasing them but no one started to line up yet. Every day, a few times a day, there were more and more posts about the All-Star Galaxy pack from various sneaker sites. They'd post about the LeBron, Kobe and KD, but still all everyone was talking about and wanted was the Foamposite. Rumour started going around that the Foamposite was the most limited shoe in the pack and that the resale value was going to be in the $1000s, maybe in the $10,000s. No one really knew.

While I was busy online reading about this, I started to get really nervous about our delivery. But then I got a call from the store saying that we got our delivery of the All Star Pack and that I could finally relax because it was finally here. I hung up the phone and raced down to the store right away. As soon as I got there one of the staff members handed me the Kobe because he knew how much of a huge Kobe fan I was, but then I immediately said, "Ok, those are cool, but let me see the Foams, where are the FOAMS?" Someone replied, "The Foams aren't here, but everything else is."

My heart sank into my boots and I freaked out. I called Nick right away and told him what was going on. He advised me to remain calm and said he'd track them down and call me right back.

An hour passed and I couldn't wait any longer so I called Nick again. There was no answer so I tried again and the same thing happened. My heart sunk as I thought for sure something had happened.

Finally, Nick called me back like four hours later and said, "Sorry, I took so long. I just had to make sure, but don't worry your Foams are at the distribution centre in Toronto, they just haven't left yet." I literally dropped to my knees and thanked the Lord, thanked him, hung up the phone and told the staff we were Ok, it just hadn't been shipped yet. We all breathed a sigh of relief and went back to work.

That relief would be short-lived.

. . .

It was a few days before the release and our lineup had already begun. Before this release, I had known almost every client who shopped at the store. We were just a little local neighbourhood shop, but that would change with this launch. The first couple of people were local repeat customers but after that it was people from all over Montreal, people I'd never seen before. In a matter of days, we went from being a local mom-and-pop shop in a small strip mall to being the hottest sneaker boutique in the city. We even got national recognitions from some Canadian sneaker blogs and as a result people from Ottawa and Toronto drove down to line up.

As I was outside talking and meeting all these new people, I met someone that had travelled all the way from New York City just to come to our release. They thought they had a better chance with us than with the New York City lines.

Things were starting to get a bit crazy.

Two days before the release, I got a call from the Montreal Gazette, which is Montreal's biggest newspaper. They told me that they heard about the lineup at my store and read all the news coming from the U.S. about this shoe. They wanted to interview me.

We were the talk of the town with the younger generation, but now with this newspaper article, everyone from all age groups would know about us.

Here is the article.

NIKE GALAXY shoe sale sees fans line up since Wednesday at Pierrefonds store

Starry-eyed Sneakerheads

ANNE SUTHERLAND
THE GAZETTE

JOHN KENNEY THE GAZETTE

Gerry Moore is at the front of the line at Pierrefonds store Exclucity, which attracted people from as far away as Long Island, N.Y., for a chance at purchasing a pair of exclusive Nike Galaxy Foamposite sneakers. Watch a video of people in the lineup at **montrealgazette/videos**

Don't call them running shoes because they won't be used for sports. Chances are they might never leave the box.

The soles glow in the dark, the uppers are a Milky Way purple, pink and blue star pattern. They are limited in number and go on sale just before this weekend's National Basketball Association All-Star game.

If you don't have them in your hands by now, chances are you never will, unless you are willing to pay way over purchase price from an Internet seller.

They are Nike Galaxy Foamposite sneakers, and the hottest item in the world of Sneakerheads, those people who covet all things sneakerish.

"Running shoes are Foot Locker – we sell lifestyle shoes; these are meant for style," said Trent, manager of the Exclucity streetwear store in Pierrefonds.

A crowd of 30 descended on Trent's store on Wednesday night for the chance to purchase a pair of the sought-after shoes that went on sale one minute after midnight Friday morning.

Jason Capinpin was close to the front of the line, sitting on a lawn chair and bundled up in duvets. He hoped his place in line would ensure him a pair of the Galaxy shoes, but wasn't sure whether he would actually wear them.

"They would be, like, too precious. I heard there were only 1,200 of them made in the world," said the Pointe Claire native.

Vanessa, no last name given, drove all the way from Long Island with a Sneakerhead friend who heard about the Montreal connection online. Fans in Manhattan have been staking out a store there for five days, so a 7¾-hour drive to Montreal didn't seem out of the question.

"I have lots of sneakers but I'm wearing my Uggs because it's cold out," she said. "After sleeping here,

I'd be upset if I didn't get a pair."

Trent had to sign an agreement with Nike not to reveal how many pairs he was getting after his store was chosen as one of the few retailers participating in the "Quick Strike," as these kinds of sales are known.

The shoes weren't even in the store on Thursday but scheduled to be delivered by a security firm late in the night.

Tiffany, who also didn't want to give her last name, and also drove up from New York, said she has more than 100 pairs of sneakers, making her a bona fide fan.

"But I wear size 2½ so it's easy for me to get them," Tiffany said.

The shoes Trent was expecting were men's sizes 8 to 13, so what will Tiff do with the pair she was hoping to score?

"I'm getting these for my boyfriend, Andrew; he doesn't know I'm doing this, so maybe I'll get a surprise with a ring."

A survey of the people waiting in line showed that 90 per cent would sell their sneakers if they got a pair, and with sellers on eBay offering shoes at $1,800 and up, it seems like a fiscally sound thing to do.

In the past, sneaker frenzy during these random sales has taken on an ugly turn.

In December, riots and mayhem broke out when the Nike Air Jordan

basketball shoes went on sale. Seattle police had to use pepper spray to control a fight that broke out in a mall where more than 1,000 people had gathered. Looters broke into a store in New York City and one rabid fan pepper-sprayed others in a line at Walmart in Los Angeles to better his chances of snagging a pair.

Trent said it's not Nike's fault; it's up to the retailer to have adequate security.

"I slept here last night and haven't left the store in two days," he said of his beard scruff.

asutherland@
montrealgazette.com

A6   ■ THE GAZETTE • montrealgazette.com • FRIDAY, FEBRUARY 24, 2012

MONTREAL

City editor: Michelle Richardson · 514-987-2463 · mlrichardson@montrealgazette.com   Assignment editor: 514-987-2637 citynews@montrealgazette.com

Bail hearing delayed in impaired-driving case

Dollard des Ormeaux man is charged with killing elderly woman, injuring husband

PAUL CHERRY
GAZETTE CRIME REPORTER

A man charged with killing an elderly woman in Dollard des Ormeaux and seriously injuring her husband, allegedly while driving impaired, saw his bail hearing delayed Thursday on the request of his lawyer.

"This is not a simple impaired-driving case," said Robert Bellefeuille, after he asked Quebec Court Judge Marie-Josée Di Lallo for permission to postpone Yvan Grandmaison's bail hearing to Tuesday.

While acknowledging the charges are serious, Bellefeuille said he wanted to be able to offer "the best guarantees possible" when he requests a release for his client.

Grandmaison, 49, of Dollard des Ormeaux, is charged with impaired driving causing the death of Bégum Wong Yee, 75, a longtime resident of D.D.O.

The charge carries a maximum life sentence upon conviction.

Grandmaison also is charged with impaired driving causing bodily harm to Wong Yee's husband, Foun Huy Shuy, 72, who was still in intensive care on Thursday.

Prosecutor Dennis Galiatsatos said Huy Shuy's injuries are considered life-threatening.

Montreal police officers who responded to the call Tuesday night suspected Grandmaison was high on drugs.

A drug recognition expert — an officer with special training — was called in and, after being inspected, Grandmaison was required to give a sample of blood or oral fluid under legislation adopted in 2008.

Preliminary results were given to Galiatsatos Thursday minutes before the bail hearing was to commence.

"I wasn't surprised by the results," was all Galiatsatos would say.

The prosecutor said cases in which the accused is charged with impaired-driving while high on drugs are becoming more common at the Montreal courthouse.

Grandmaison was convicted in 2004 at the Valleyfield courthouse in an impaired-driving case.

He was fined $600 and sentenced to one year of supervised probation.

In 2006, he was charged again with impaired driving, but was acquitted in 2008.

Bellefeuille said many factors can come into play in an impaired-driving case, including where the vehicles were standing at the time of the accident.

For example, judges in impaired-driving cases involving whether a sober person would have struck a person under the same circumstances. In 2005, a judge in Valleyfield convicted a man of driving while well over the legal blood-alcohol limit but acquitted him of killing a 12-year-old boy. The court heard evidence the boy suddenly moved toward the middle of the road on his bike when he was hit.

In Grandmaison's case, a neighbour of the victim told The Gazette residents are forced to walk in the street in the winter because there are no sidewalks.

The matter could be part of the case, said Bellefeuille, adding his client called 911 after the accident.

"Witnesses said he was panicking as much as he couldn't talk."

pcherry@
montrealgazette.com

NIKE GALAXY shoe sale sees fans line up since Wednesday at Pierrefonds store

Starry-eyed Sneakerheads

ANNE SUTHERLAND
THE GAZETTE

Don't call them running shoes because they won't be used for sport. Chances are they might never leave the box.

The soles glow in the dark, the uppers are a milky way purple, pink and blue star pattern. They are limited in number and go on sale just before this weekend's National Basketball Association All-Star game.

If you don't have them in your hands by now, chances are you never will, unless you are willing to pay way over purchase price from an Internet seller.

They are Nike Galaxy Foamposite sneakers, and the hottest item in the world of Sneakerheads, those people who covet all things sneakerish.

"Running shoes are Foot Locker — we sell lifestyle shoes, these are meant for style," said Trent, manager of the Exclucity streetwear store in Pierrefonds.

A crowd of 50 descended on Trent's store on Wednesday night for the chance to purchase a pair of the sought-after shoes that went on sale one minute after midnight Friday morning.

Jason Capinegro was close to the front of the line, sitting on a lawn chair and handled up in throws. He hoped his place in the line would ensure him a pair of the Galaxy shoes, but wasn't sure whether he would actually wear them.

"They would be, like, too precious. I heard there were only 1,200 of them made in the world," said the Pointe Claire native.

Vanessa, no last name given, drove all the way from Long Island with a Sneakerhead friend who heard about the Montreal connection online. Fans in Manhattan have been staking out a store there for five days, so a 7½-hour drive to Montreal didn't win out of the question.

"I have lots of sneakers but I'm wearing my Uggs because it's cold out," she said. "After sleeping here, I'd be upset if I didn't get a pair."

Trent had to sign an agreement with Nike not to reveal how many pairs he was getting after his store was chosen as one of the few retailers participating in the "Quick Strike" to these kinds of sales are known.

The shoes weren't even in the store on Thursday but expected to be delivered by a security firm late in the night.

"Tiffany, who also didn't want to give her last name, and also drove up from New York, said she has more than 100 pairs of sneakers, making hers a bona fide fan.

"But I wear size 5½ so it's easy for me to get them," Tiffany said.

The shoes Trent was expecting were men's sizes 8 to 13, so what will Tiff do with the pair she was hoping to score?

"I'm getting these for my boyfriend, Andrew; he doesn't know I'm doing this, so maybe I'll get a surprise with a ring."

A survey of the people waiting in line showed all 90 per cent would sell their sneakers if they got a pair, and with sellers on eBay offering shoes at $1,800 and up, it seems the attraction wasn't that hard to do.

In December, riots and mayhem broke out when the Nike Air Jordan basketball shoes went on sale. Seattle police had to use pepper spray to control a fight that broke out in a mall where more than 1,000 people had gathered. Looters broke into a store in New York City and one raced for pepper-sprayed others in a line at Walmart in Los Angeles to better his chances of snagging a pair.

Trent said it's not Nike's fault; it's up to the retailer to have adequate security.

"I hope here last night and haven't left the store in two days," he said of he herself.

asutherland@
montrealgazette.com

Gerry Moore is at the front of the line at Pierrefonds store Exclucity, which attracted people from as far away as Long Island, N.Y., for a chance at purchasing a pair of exclusive Nike Galaxy Foamposite sneakers. Watch a video of people in the lineup at montrealgazette.com/videos

---

February to turn wintry

Snow followed by relatively cooler weather is in top for Friday and this weekend.

The expected wintry weather comes amid a particularly dry and mild February.

Environment Canada forecasts 10 to 15 centimetres of snow for the Montreal region starting Friday morning.

It could be snowy since the temperature will hover around 0C, according to Environment Canada meteorologist André Cantin. The air will chill to minus 6C Friday night.

"It really will be snow and it will stay" on the ground, Cantin said.

Another 10 cm is forecast for the Montreal region for Monday evening into Tuesday, he added.

"We might yet catch up with February averages."

The average February snowfall for the Montreal region is 43 cm. As of Wednesday, the total stood at 38 cm.

The average temperature for the month is minus 6.6C. Between Feb. 1 and Feb. 22, it was minus 4.4C.

Including Thursday, 12 days in February — more than half were 0C or warmer.

Temperatures Saturday and Sunday will rise to highs of 0C or minus 1C, cooler than the balmy high of 9C on Wednesday.

THE GAZETTE

■ In the NEWS

POLICE SEEKING POTENTIAL VICTIMS

Police are seeking potential victims of a man alleged to have threatened to publish photos of a sexual assault with a 15-year-old girl on the Internet unless she paid him not to. Troy Dottin, 30, was arrested Feb. 11 by Montreal police. He faces charges of sexual assault, production and possession of juvenile pornography, sexual contact with a minor, invitation to sexual touching, extortion and uttering death threats, police said. Dottin is alleged to have had sex with a 15-year-old girl and photographed and videotaped the encounter. Police then threatened to put the images online unless the teen gave him money, police said.

PEDESTRIAN DIES AFTER BEING HIT

A 62-year-old woman died in hospital Thursday after being hit by a car at about 11 a.m. while walking across a street on a green light in Ahuntsic. She was crossing Fleury/Faubourg Ave. at Fleury St., near Montreal police Constable Yannick Ouimet said. The vehicle was travelling on Fleury and was making a left turn on a green light on to Papineau, he added. "The driver did not see the pedestrian," Ouimet added. The driver of the car, a 51-year-old woman, was treated for shock. There will be no charges laid, police confirmed.

DRUG RING BUST NETS 18 PEOPLE

Police arrested 18 people on Wednesday and Thursday in an operation to bust a drug ring in the city's east end. Police did not release the information until Thursday so as not to compromise the operation, said Montreal police Constable Yannick Ouimet. Those arrested range in age from 43 to 47.

THE GAZETTE

Tuition-hike protesters come face to face with cops in riot gear

THE GAZETTE

Students demonstrating against tuition hikes shut down the Jacques Cartier Bridge for more than 50 minutes during Thursday's afternoon rush-hour, as a protest organizer said about 15,000 marched through downtown Montreal.

The bridge shutdown was caused when about 300 protesters left Place Émilie-Gamelin by the René-Lévesque métro station, where it looked like the main protest was about to break up.

"To the bridge! To the bridge!" the marchers chanted.

Shadowed by police and under the watch of a news helicopter, they made their way to Delorimier Ave. and de Maisonneuve Blvd., where they were confronted by Montreal police in riot gear at about 4 p.m.

After a few minutes of trying to stare each other down, police told the marchers they were now engaged in an illegal protest, and they headed east along Ste. Catherine St.

But a second group of marchers had made its way to Cartier St., about a block west of the standoff, and almost managed to get to the northbound lanes leading to the bridge.

They were confronted by more Montreal police who, clashing their night-sticks as they held up their shields, drove the protesters away from the span.

The confrontation led the Sûreté du Québec, which is responsible for patrolling the bridge, to set up its own line of riot police across the span. The demonstrators dispersed only to rally once more at Place Émilie-Gamelin, where the march eventually broke up at about 6:30 p.m.

Police said one person was arrested.

Students shut down the Jacques Cartier Bridge for more than 50 minutes during Thursday's afternoon rush-hour.

MARIE-FRANCE COALLIER THE GAZETTE

Did you catch the line in that article about the shoes not being there? Of course, the reporter wanted to see the Foams, but I HAD NO IDEA WHERE THE HELL THEY WERE BECAUSE THEY HADN'T BEEN DELIVERED YET.

It was Wednesday, two days before the release, and there were about 30 to 40 people outside and more coming every hour. At this point, I still had no idea if we were going to get the Foams on time, or if we would even get them at all.

I did the only thing I could do; I called Nick.

I told him that I just lied to the Gazette by saying that Nike is delivering them with a security firm because I couldn't think of anything else to say. Nick listened to my rant and then he said, "Trent, I'm sorry, I'll look into it right away and call you right back."

Nick called a few minutes later and told me that my foams were still in the warehouse. Nike would get the shoes to me by express air shipping which would deliver them the next day without fail. I told him that I didn't want to take the chance and that I would drive to Toronto right away and get them myself. He called his boss to get approval but that wasn't allowed, so I had no choice but to sit and wait for the delivery.

I didn't sleep that night and spent all day on Thursday at the front door of the store waiting to see that damn UPS truck. By Thursday 4pm, there was still no delivery so I called Nick again to tell him that they still hadn't arrived, and that I had no choice but to cancel the release.

I wasn't going to let people sleep outside in the cold another night, knowing that there was a chance that we weren't going to get the foams. But Nick begged me not to do that because he was confident that he could fix the situation. He asked me to wait until the morning before I make any announcements.

The next morning was Friday and we were 15 hours away from release. Nick called me to tell me that my Galaxy Foams were still in the Nike system, meaning that they were still in the distribution centre. But wait, it gets better. This time, instead of asking the warehouse to confirm that they were there, Nick asked his brother, who was also a Nike sales rep in Toronto, to go to the warehouse and physically check himself to ensure 100% that they were, in fact, still there. Reps don't usually have access to the warehouse like that but this was an emergency.

I thanked Nick and asked him to call me right away when he got any news, good or bad.

Nick called me back around 1:30 p.m., exactly 10 hours and 30 minutes before release. "I've got good news for you. We found your foamposites. My brother is physically at the site and he's not letting those Foams out of his sight."

I think I literally started crying.

I was so ecstatic that I didn't even know what to do with myself. I remember being in shock. I was processing but still not comprehending; it was just so confusing. I was happy but I also knew that we still had a huge problem on our hands. We were 10 hours away from release and the Foams were still in Toronto. I didn't know if we could get them out of the warehouse ourselves in time to make the release. I was beside myself but Nick's brother had a plan.

While Nick was trying to figure what to do next, his brother called him back and said, "Yo, I got the Foams in my car, I'm going home to change my clothes and then I'm heading down to Montreal. Tell Trent not to worry, he'll have his Foams on time for release at midnight."

When Nick told me what his brother was doing, I was in total shock. I couldn't believe what Nick was even saying. I think I asked him to repeat himself about ten times.

I'm literally indebted to Nick's brother for the rest of my life.

. . .

Nike has a very tight wall of secrecy that is impossible to break, even with accounts that they are close with. Till this day, I still don't know what happened to those Foamposites and why they were never shipped out to me on time. Nick and his brother still won't tell me. They claim they don't know but I don't believe them. Of course, they know. Lol! I think someone somewhere was trying to be slick.

Regardless of all that, Nick's brother arrived with the Galaxy Foamposites two hours before our midnight release. None of the people outside had a clue what was going on, only my staff and I knew. And I'm not going to tell you how we snuck them inside past everyone because I might have to do it again some day.

. . .

At midnight, February 25, 2012, we released the Nike All Star Galaxy pack. At the time of the release, there were about 150 to 200 people outside. Channel 12 News, the fire department and about six cop cars were also present that night; it was a circus.

As crazy as things were, we fortunately had a great release and there were no incidents, fights or arrests.

After the release was over, I had everyone wait around outside and I held an auction for the last pair of Galaxy Foamposites. The cops weren't very happy about it but it was for a good cause. There was a little Black girl in the neighbourhood that had just been diagnosed with cancer and her parent didn't have money for her treatments. I ran the auction myself outside our front door. We raised a lot of money for her and everyone left on a happy note. Of course, there were some people who were bitter because they didn't get anything, but that's all part of the game.

Most people didn't buy The LeBron, Kobe or KD, because everyone was so fixated on the Foamposite. But that was a huge mistake because all three of those shoes are worth triple or more of their retail price today on the resale market. They could have made a lot of money.

. . .

We had a great release but that wasn't the same for some sneaker stores in the USA where it caused complete mayhem. The worst was in Florida where the actual NBA All-Star Game was being held; they had to call in the National Guard.

After the weekend madness, the Monday morning news wasn't entirely positive for Nike. Every news agency across North America covered this story but also faulted Nike for putting kids at risk for trying to get these limited-edition shoes.

At the end of the Montreal Gazette's article where the reporter listed some other Nike releases that got some backlash, I said, "It's not Nike's fault, it's up to the retailer to have adequate security." Well, Nike caught wind of the article and loved that part the most.

That same day, I sent Nike a recap email filled with pictures of our releases, the Gazette's article and a link to a video of us on the news. Don't forget that during our release, in the midst of all this chaos, the store was fully decorated. We had someone walking around inside and outside the store in a freaking astronaut costume taking pics with clients while handing out coffee and doughnuts to the people in line. Our pics were amazing. No other store had done that and I wanted to make sure Nike was aware of what I was doing.

My email went around the offices of the Nike World Headquarters like wildfire. It put the Exclucity brand top of mind with some of Nike's biggest executives.

That Nike All Star Pack release was the first huge major **brand** moment for Exclucity. And it happened as a result of hard work, taking chances, and most importantly, creating something organic, authentic and sustainable that connected with my clients. That's not to be taken lightly. I heard of stores that got that pack but did nothing with it. I took the opportunity to build on the moment because I cared more about my **brand** than I did about the profits.

Fun Fact:

Someone that was in our lineup and bought a Galaxy Foamposite sold the pair on eBay for $90,000, but the e-commerce corporation removed it and voided the sale. I'm not sure why or what transpired after that but the guy sued eBay and won.

. . .

Nike

A group of Nike executives from Portland was coming to visit the Montreal area to do market travel and Nick was excited about bringing them to the store. These were some of the same execs from Vegas, Jim Wood, Mark Fox, Will Shelby and a few others. This was going to be the first time they were coming to see me on my turf. Las Vegas is a good place to meet and talk to execs but there are a bunch of other accounts around. This was my opportunity to showcase my **brand** to them one-on-one.

When they arrived at the store, I could see the look on their faces as they got out the SUVs. They were amazed that the Exclucity they heard so much about was being operated out of a small strip mall in the middle of suburbia. Nick told them not to be alarmed as he thought the same thing when he first drove up but they should wait until they got inside.

As they walked in the looks on their faces went from confusion to smiles and they all started bobbing their heads to the Hip Hop I had bumping through the speakers.

Don't forget all these people were American, and at that time I was still living in Queens, New York, and brought back inventory for the store every week. Most of the apparel in the store came from Brooklyn, Queens, and Manhattan so the store had a familiar feel and vibe to it.

They felt like they were back home.

The pics I had put up around the store that I had taken with celebrities also caught their attention. From modelling and being in the music industry, I had taken tonnes of pics with celebs like T.I., Soulja Boy, Alicia Keys, Serena and Venus Williams, Beanie Sigel, Bun B, and even Hillary Clinton.

Jim Wood (the big boss), the one I was talking to in Vegas about the Foams took one look at the wall and out of all those high-profile celebs he asked me about Bun B. Bun B is a rap legend from Houston, Texas, for anyone reading this who doesn't know rap.

Jim, who is an old white man, turns to me and says, "Bun B, that's my boy," in the heaviest southern Texas accent you've ever heard. He then took out his phone and called Bun B right in front of me. That built our bond even more.

At the time, the location of the store was the thing that made me the most nervous about that Nike visit. I was afraid these big executives were going to say, "We can't have our most premium products going to a store in a strip mall, in the middle of nowhere." But it did the opposite. The location was the thing that they admired the most about the store. They were so impressed that I was able to create something so impactful in the middle of nowhere that we started talking about expanding right then and there.

Jim said to me, "This is really something unique that you got here. It's really impressive, but can you scale it?" The store was all about me, my style, and my vibe, but he was asking me if I could replicate it.

What is a scaling strategy?

*Growth means adding resources at the same rate that you're adding revenue. ... **Scaling** growth is about creating business models and designing your organization in a way that easily scales in order to generate consistent revenue growth and avoid stall-points without adding a tonne of extra costs and/or resources along the way.*

A business isn't really a business if you can't scale it and one day sell it for a multiple. Jim wasn't saying that I had to open more stores, he was just opening my eyes to the possibility and pushing me to be better.

Nike will never tell you what to do with your brand, but they will let you know if they support your vision and if they align with your goals.

After that day, I knew I had Nike's full support but the big question was, what did I want, what were my goals?

The truth is, at that exact time, I wasn't sure. Scaling a business would require 100% of my attention and if I wanted to do it right, I'd have to quit modelling. I had just recently broken into the US modelling market and things were going so well for me that I had no idea what to do. I was at a crossroads.

On one hand, I had modelling but I was starting to get a bit tired of the bullshit that goes on in that world. Being signed to a modelling agency is like being on basketball team and there aren't many positions on the roster for Black models. For every ten white male models, they only needed one Black model.

On the other hand, you have Nike that never rejected me and they welcomed my Blackness. Nike knows I'm of the culture and that is something that can't be taught. Nike appreciated that and wanted me to expand on it. Having Nike's full support was an opportunity that I couldn't let pass me by.

All of my years of struggling, working 7 days a week and 18-hour days had brought me to this point. I was also fully aware that if I used this opportunity correctly, I could be the first person in my family to start building generational wealth and change my entire family's cycle forever.

. . .

I, of course, chose Exclucity over modelling and decided to start scaling my business and opening more stores. This was what my grandmothers and parents came to this country for; this was my purpose.

It was time for me to start building a brand.

. . .

If I hadn't gotten the opportunity with Nike, there's no telling where I'd end up. Maybe I would have made it in modelling but maybe I would have gone back and made stupid decisions like when I was young, dumb and ignorant. I'll never know but I do know one thing. I'll be forever grateful and indebted to Nike for the opportunity.

. . .

Scaling

Since Exclucity was now known in the city because of the All Star release, and I had Nike's full support, I started actively looking for a space in downtown Montreal to open my second location. After all that attention from the release, I knew time was of the essence. I had to capitalize on the momentum.

After a few weeks of looking around, I found a great space just outside the heart of downtown Montreal in Griffintown. I was still downtown but it was just off the beaten path; it was perfect.

Like the lease that I signed for my first location, I was again very nervous about signing a second lease for this new location. This was an even bigger commitment and this lease was so much more expensive because it was downtown.

I fought off the nerves, signed the lease and started planning for an October 20, 2012 opening.

For the upcoming months, my plan was to work on my new store concept and get things ready for the grand opening, but Nike had other plans. 2012 would be the year that changed the sneaker industry forever; the next few months were going to be very busy.

. . .

Nike Air Yeezy Release

A few weeks after the Galaxy release, Nike announced the June 9 release of the Nike Air Yeezy 2 Pure Platinum and Solar Red, and people lost their minds. Someone started camping outside of a store in L.A two months before the release date. Nike had gotten a lot of backlash from the All Star release so when they heard about this they put some new restrictions in place to avoid the mass hysteria from happening again.

The new restrictions didn't lessen the hype one bit as everyone still wanted those Yeezys, but they made things safer and that LA line was cancelled.

In the U.S., the colours were split by coast. I think the East Coast got Solar Red and the West Coast got Pure Platinum, but there were so few stores in Canada getting them that those that did got both. Exclucity was included on that very exclusive list of stores.

The purpose for releases, like the Nike Air Yeezy and the All Star pack, is to draw attention to both Nike and the store that is carrying them. It's not so much about making money. The pairs are so limited that there is no big profit to be made but the attention is priceless. Knowing that this

Nike Air Yeezy release would draw a lot of attention, I tried to think of ways to outdo our Galaxy Foamposite release so we'd stand out.

Keeping it fun and inexpensive, I decided to really play up on the Kanye and Kim celebrity element. They had just started dating in 2011 so they were the hot couple at the time, they arguably still are. I rented a big red carpet to roll out and metal poles with the red velvet ropes, just like the ones they use at award shows and in VIP sections. I rented a small stage with red drapes to use as a backdrop. I got two people from my staff to dress up like Kim and Kanye. I printed pictures of Kim and Kanye that I found on the Internet and made masks for the two staff members to wear.

BOOM, there you go, "Kanye" and "Kim" were at our Nike Air Yeezy release.

We also asked everyone coming to bring their favourite Kanye West CD. To get in the door and past the velvet ropes, they had to rap a line from their favourite Kanye song, kind of like the secret code to get into VIP.

It was really something to see.

Those who got a pair of Nike Air Yeezys that day got to take a pic with our fake Kanye and Kim in the VIP lounge. People loved it. I didn't spend more than $1000, but it was one of the most memorable moments in Exclucity's history.

. . .

Everything went really well that day except for the fact that a man with a gun tried to rob someone in line and almost ruined the day for everyone.

The rumour is that someone in line had sold their space to him and taken his money but then changed their mind a few hours before release. The guy got pissed off, went home and got a gun.

All I saw from inside the store was a commotion and as I was about to step out to see what was going on, I saw four cop cars speeding into the parking lot. The cops jumped out of their cars, drew their guns, and yelled, "Freeze, don't move."

I was sure this guy was going to take off running but all he started yelling was, "Yo, who snitched, who snitched?" I think he didn't run because the guy who he was beefing with had all his info. I have no idea. All I know is the cops put him on the ground, searched him and found the gun.

The cops stopped the event, questioned me and a few other people in line and after their investigation we were allowed to continue with the release. The rest of the day was flawless. I held another auction, this time to raise money to buy basketballs and studio equipment for the youth centre.

I had avoided what could have been a huge disaster that day, but most importantly, no one was hurt and all was well in the sneaker community.

I put all the fake Kanye and Kim pics in a deck, sent it to Nike, and again my email was forwarded to all the execs at its World Headquarters. It was a grand slam hit, and again Nike couldn't have been happier with me.

I also put the pics on a new social media platform that was gaining popularity, Instagram. It was 2012 and social media was about to explode and I was right there ready for it.

. . .

Social Media

The Gram started in 2010, BUT it really didn't start popping till 2012, and I was all over it. I'd post all of our releases on there, but I also posted all of our clients buying their shoes as well, and mention them. It was a thing we were known for back then. Customers would buy shoes and ask, "Are you going to take my picture and put it on Instagram?"

It was the beginning of the social media era and I capitalized off of it in a major way.

Today, when people ask me about my strategy and how I built a brand, I tell them the truth. Everything I did was organically done because I was broke. I had no other options but I think that's the best way. Necessity is the mother of invention so it made me think outside the box, that's what made it so effective. Today, people just think that they can throw money at something and make it work.

That's not how I did it.

From I first started the store in the basement, I barely had enough money for rent and inventory so there was definitely no money for marketing and promotion. When I was selling Long Tees from the trunk of my car, I had people's cell phone numbers, and if I didn't have their cell number, I asked them for the next best thing, their MSN!

Back in the day, having someone's MSN was even better than having their phone number because you couldn't send pictures and videos with your cell phone, but you could send pics over MSN Messenger.

Whenever I got back from NYC with the new inventory, the first thing I did the next day was to take pics and send them to my clients on

MSN. It wasn't a brilliant marketing strategy that I paid a marketing firm to come up with but it worked. I used MSN to talk to my friends so I just flipped it and used it for business cuz it was free. The concept might seem like the norm now because now every store is on social media, but back in the day trust me, there were no stores talking and replying to clients on MSN Messenger.

Back then I didn't only use MSN Messenger I also Hi5 and Myspace. If there were any new social platforms, I'd open a personal account and also one for Exclucity. I was using social media for business so early that Facebook flagged me for it and tried to shut my page down.

At first, Facebook's mission was to connect college kids with other college kids. This grew to connecting people with other people but the point is Facebook was for people only, people with faces. Businesses weren't allowed to use it for their purposes.

I couldn't care less what they said, I needed a new way to connect with my clients. Everyone was leaving MSN and Myspace and moving to Facebook so I had to move with them. I started an Exclucity Facebook page, regardless.

Everything was going fine, however, a few months later I got an email from Facebook that they were closing my page because I broke the guidelines. I thought I was going to die.

MSN, Hi5 and Myspace were all dead and everyone was on Facebook. I had no other way to communicate with my clients and get all the new styles out.

In the body of the e-mail, Facebook also said, "Even though we're closing your account, you won't lose your friends. We will transfer all of them over to a new feature that we are starting called Pages. At the time, I had no idea wtf Pages was, but as we all know today Pages is huge and is one of Facebook's most used features.

Exclucity was one of the first on Facebook Pages.

I read a few years ago that Facebook started Pages because of a request that Starbucks made. Apparently, Pages worked well for Starbucks so Facebook decided to start testing it out on a few other accounts (like Exclucity).

. . .

In my opinion, Facebook made social media what it is today, but if you ask me, Instagram changed our lives, forever.

In 2012, people used Facebook on their desktop or laptops, which meant you had to wait until you were at your computer to interact and use it.

Instagram was always a phone app, you never really use Instagram on your computer. Your phone is always with you and you are always on your phone, that's why I think Instagram got bigger than Facebook. (Yes, I know Facebook owns Instagram for anyone that's saying that to me in their head.)

I was on Instagram every second of every day interacting with our clients, liking pics and posting about Exclucity. I'd post peoples dogs when they brought them into the store and when someone came in with cool kicks on. I also posted when the UPS guy showed up with our delivery and our staff doing stupid shit and goofing around. I was nonstop with it; I posted everything.

Today, all of this is normal; companies hire for social media positions and people make huge amount of money just to do all this stuff.

They are hired to make it all look natural and organic, but back then I was doing it because it was fun to do. It was a cool way to connect with my clients and it was FREE. I had no idea what I was doing at the time but it totally put us on the map because people loved it.

Exclucity's Instagram was notorious.

. . .

LeBron South Beach Release

Our next big release after the Nike Air Yeezy was the LeBron 9 P.S. Elite "South Beach." The LeBron 8 "South Beach" will forever be the classic, but Nike was trying to ride the wave. This release was not going to be on the same level of hype as the Galaxy or Air Yeezy release, but it was still going to be big.

I wanted to do something different this time, but I wasn't sure what to do. Since the madness of the Foamposite release, Nike had banned midnight releases so we could only do a release at 8am but that gave me an idea.

Prior to the LeBron release, I had always bought coffee and doughnuts for the people in line, had the staff hand them out, and I always encouraged the staff to talk with the people in line and be friendly. For this release, I considered taking that up a notch and doing it bigger.

This release would be a customer appreciation event and we were gonna have a party.

The release was on a Saturday morning so Friday at 9pm instead of closing the store like we usually do, I did something a bit different.

The staff made it look like we were closing; then went outside to say goodbye to everyone in line. At the last minute before we turn the lights off, I had the staff go back outside and surprise everyone by inviting them inside for a PARTY! We technically closed the store; the cash was closed, but everyone who was in line outside got to come in for a party. We had the basketball game on as it was playoff time and we also had music, food, snacks and some drinks. We had board games, cards and Dominions. It was like a house party.

Everyone loved it.

Around 2am, we turned off the music and pretended we were closing down for real this time and that everyone would have to go back outside. But that's when we surprised them again. We turned the music back on, brought out sleeping bags and tents, and announced that the entire staff would be sleeping over at the store. The customers could stay inside with us if they wanted.

It was the funniest sight ever. People were sleeping on tables and using tees and jeans as pillows. Some people just slept right there on the floor, it was amazing. It was one of my favourite releases ever.

In the morning, the staff cleaned everything up and then transformed the store into Miami South Beach. I think we got a bit of sand, but I know for sure I got this cheesy summer beach backdrop so in the pictures you'd see a fake Miami backdrop as a joke. I also got a bunch of those weird/funny sunglasses from the party store for them to use in the pictures as well.

We took pics and I posted the event all over social media and also sent it to Nike on Monday morning. It was another smash.

2012 was Exclucity's year. We couldn't miss.

. . .

Market Travel

A few weeks had passed since our last big release and there weren't any major releases coming up soon so I decided to take a little trip.

Before opening my 2nd location, I wanted to do a bit of market research travel and visit the top 10 sneaker boutiques in the U.S. to try to understand what made them excel.

I wanted to know where they were located, what their store layout looked like, what colours they used and anything else that could help me. I also wanted to know about their staff; how knowledgeable were they about the products they were selling, how they dressed, and most importantly, how did they serve the clients. I not only wanted to learn from them, but to see what their flaws were so Exclucity could be better.

This is something I still do until today. I've visited sneaker boutiques across the globe to enrich my knowledge and stay ahead of the game.

. . .

I flew to New York, visited a bunch of shops there and then drove to New Jersey and Philadelphia. At first, I just wanted to see the top 10 boutiques but soon figured that since I'm there I might as well see them all. I must have visited 50 or more stores that week. I looked at the biggest and the smallest. I visited the big-box stores and also the mom-and-pop ones.

I learned a lot on the trip and got a tonne of ideas for Exclucity, but my research didn't stop there.

One of my friends that worked at Nike World Headquarters in Beaverton, Oregon had given me an open invitation to visit the campus anytime. I had always wanted to so that I could learn more about Nike and pick the brains of some of the great people working there. The timing was perfect.

. . .

When I arrived at the Beaverton headquarters, I got a formal tour of the entire campus, which takes about a full day. I got to see Michael Jordan's original signed contract, all his game-worn shoes, the Tiger Woods and Serena Williams building, and a bunch of other cool things. It was quite mind-blowing.

I visited the campus a few more times over the years, but the first one will always stick out to me the most. I got to meet and talk to so many people who make the brand move daily. It was an honour.

I learned the Nike DNA and how they got started, which, ironically, is the same way that Exclucity began. Nike started selling sneakers from the trunk of a car to athletes. They have a replica of Bill Bowerman's car on campus with shoeboxes in the trunk; it's really cool.

Nike even had a name change in the beginning years, just like Exclucity did. Nike was originally called Blue Ribbon Sports.

I learned a lot on this trip but one piece of advice stuck out to me the most. It's advice that I use until today and I apply it to everything I do, even in my personal life.

During my tour, I asked an exec what's one piece of advice he could give me to help grow Exclucity. He said, "Make Nike need you, not the other way around."

That is the most powerful piece of advice I think I've ever gotten in my life. It is why Nike is by far the best and biggest sports brand in the world. Nike aligns itself with the best of the best, with leaders, and with the most dominant athletes and stores in the world.

You can't wait around for someone to validate you; you have to create your own lane. When you're undeniable, the world will come to you, not the other way around.

. . .

Downtown Montreal, 2nd Location

My October 20, 2012, grand opening was fast approaching and I was a bit nervous but I was ready for it. I had planned out a solid restock and when I announced it there was a lot of buzz in the city. This relaxed my nerves a lot.

I certainly didn't invent the strategy of 'restocking,' but I made it popular in Montreal at the time. Simply put, it had never been done to the levels that I did it.

For those of you who aren't in the sneaker world, let me explain what 'restocking' means. By now, I'm sure you understand the Nike strategy. It's simple; make it limited and build the hype. The more limited a release is, the more people will want it.

A 'restock' means bringing back some of those hyped limited releases from the past year or so and rereleasing them. If you think people go crazy for the original release, imagine restocking them and giving people one more chance at getting them again at retail price.

Restocking is typically reserved for new store openings to help bring the most attention possible to the opening of that new location. It's a strategy that I not only popularized in Montreal but I held a restock so big that I got in trouble for it from Nike. (More on that later.)

One of my other strategies for store openings was to make them a surprise, which added to the hype.

People would go to some serious lengths to find out where our new store locations were so that they could be first inline and have first dibs on the restock. But I'd go to greater lengths to hide it from them.

From the day that I got the keys to the 2nd location, I'd park a few blocks away and walk to the store with glasses and a hat on. Since we announced the opening and restock, we received hundreds of calls and emails asking us where the new location was but we told them that we'd announce it on Instagram only a few hours before opening.

I thought it would be cool to have everybody rush down but my clients had different plans. People were on a mission to find the location so they could start lining up early.

I had been going to the store for about two months to set things up, but always in disguise. Everything was cool, except for when I messed up just two days before the opening. I went to the damn corner store for five minutes without my disguise and got caught.

Someone yelled out my name "Trent". I shouldn't have turned around, but when you hear your name instinct kicks in and you automatically turn around. One of our clients saw me, run up to me and asked, "Is this where the new store is going to be?" I tried to deny it and said it was my friend's store but he wasn't buying it for one second.

The guy stayed there and started to line up in front of the store. He then posted the address on Instagram and more people started coming.

The funny thing is that same guy ended up being the first person inline at our next two store openings as well. He even changed his IG account name to @firstinline (Someone else has that account name now, so don't try to search for it.)

The opening of our 2nd location was amazing. The entire Montreal sneaker community came out and it was a day for Montreal to come together and celebrate. Montreal finally had a sneaker boutique in the downtown area. There were other stores in Montreal that carried sneakers but none that were dedicated to sneakers and sneaker culture, and that carried an assortment as broad as we did.

. . .

Over the next year, with two locations open, I continued with the same recipe. We were known for getting every hype sneaker release and building a fun event around it and getting those hype shoes into the hands of the real sneakerheads.

For the Nike Foamposites "Army" print, we had a push-up competition between our clients at both of our stores. Whoever did the most push-ups won a free pair of Foams.

We held a Ladies' Night for the Women's Nike Air Max 1 "City pack." We had a hairdresser, manicurist, masseuse, and a mini fashion show at the store and all the women left with a gift bag of coupons and other goodies.

For Nike LeBron 10 "Cork," we had a staff member at each location dress up in a full butler uniform and bring the people inline their shoes on a silver platter with a glass of champagne.

We turned both locations into a space station for the Nike 2013 All Star Pack, a step-up from 2012. We had an electronic basketball game, smoke machines, a light show and aliens were everywhere.

We had so many activations that I couldn't list them all. There were over thirty of them and as usual we put them up on social media; it's what we were known for.

Exclucity was beyond just sneakers.

. . .

Just a note for anyone that might be reading this and thinking about becoming an entrepreneur. The best question to ask yourself before you start or open any new business is, "Are you solving a problem?"

You don't have to revolutionize an industry to be successful but you should be trying to solve a problem. Uber is a great example of a business that solved a problem. Uber didn't invent taxi service; they just made it easier and more convenient for you to get a cab.

Exclucity wasn't the first sneaker boutique in the world and it won't be the last, but I did solve a problem. I brought in the broadest sneaker assortment in the city and I gave female sneakerheads a place where they felt included. This was a fun environment where everyone felt welcomed as opposed to the old elitist sneaker boutiques that catered to clients owning massive collections.

I made shopping for sneakers fun, exciting and feel less transactional. Similar to the feeling you get when you walk into an Apple store.

. . .

Planning Ahead & Negotiating Leases

Nike or other brands will never tell you what to do with your brand but they will encourage and support you if your brand aligns with their plans. As I was deep diving into scaling my business, Nike was looking to clean up the marketplace and work with premium retailers and expand sneaker culture outside of the U.S., in places like Canada. Our growth plans aligned.

My first store was in the West Island of Montreal, and I had just opened one in the downtown area, so my next logical move was to open an Exclucity in the south of Montreal and then the north. I knew that if I wanted to expand across Canada, I would have to prove myself to Nike and the other brands first, and be successful in Montreal.

I set out to open my next two stores quickly.

My real estate agent found me a location in the South Shore; an outdoor mall in the city of Brossard. At the same time, he also found a location in the north in an outdoor mall in the city of Laval. I liked the locations so I figured I'd negotiate both leases at the same time, which would give me more leverage (mentally).

Here's a "Cheat code": When negotiating anything, try not to want it. If you really want or need something the other side will smell that and then you're already starting at a disadvantage. Negotiating both leases at the same time not only gave me mental leverage but I also learned something with the Laval lease negotiation that I applied to the Brossard one, which would come in handy later on.

There was a store in the Laval mall that sold jogging shoes and had an exclusivity clause on footwear in their lease. An exclusivity clause protects you from competition. I really wanted to rent this location so I fought the clause. I knew that our business wouldn't affect each other and, if anything, Exclucity could help their business by bringing more traffic to the area.

They sold running shoes to marathon runners. I used to shop there when I was running marathons, which proves my point, our product didn't overlap. If I shopped there for shoes, that meant Exclucity didn't carry those shoes. I just had to get that message to them.

I got the contact info for the CEO of the store and I wouldn't leave him alone until he lifted his exclusivity clause and let me in the mall. It would take some time to get it done, but I eventually got him to lift it. He was a fair man, and once he understood what I was saying he had no problem with it.

Armed with this new knowledge about an exclusivity clause in malls, I went straight to the lawyers that where handling the Brossard lease and told them that I wanted to add a clause before signing.

I wanted exclusivity on shoes in the Brossard mall.

The mall and the lawyers quickly rejected my request but I didn't want to give up that easily. I made another attempt for exclusivity but this time on basketball shoes. No one sold basketball shoes in the mall so I knew it would be more difficult for them to say no.

"The Uniform Boys," who specialize in basketball shoes, weren't in the mall yet but I knew one day they would try, especially after we opened there. If I got this clause approved and put in my lease, the landlord would have to ask my permission to allow them to open in the mall if they ever wanted to be there.

When my lawyer called me to say that the mall had accepted my exclusivity clause on basketball shoes, I told him I wanted to sign right away before they realize what they had just given up and change their mind.

I signed the lease that day and made plans to open on December 7, 2013.

. . .

South Shore, The 3ʳᵈ Location

The Brossard opening went as scheduled and it was bigger and better than the downtown opening. I had a huge restock but this time I took it up a notch. With the help of Nike's marketplace director, Barb Frank, I was able to have Gentry Humphrey host the opening for me.

I'm sure most of you don't know who he is but just Google his name if you want more details. Gentry Humphrey is a living legend in the sneaker world and has worked closely with Michael Jordan for over 30 years. He's a big deal.

Having Gentry host the opening for me didn't only help raise awareness about the opening and the Exclucity brand, but it also got the attention of a few Nike execs from Nike Toronto's head office. A few of them came down to support the opening.

. . .

Since having my Nike account, I've had four marketplace directors and had an amazing relationship with each of them. Will Shelby was my first and gave me the fundamentals and insight that I needed to learn to work better with Nike. Will was also the one who introduced me to Jim Wood and it was both of them that approved my expansion plans.

Then there was Barb Frank who was more like a big sister. Not only did Barb help me get Gentry to the Brossard opening but she also introduced me to a bunch of Nike execs, and pushed the Exclucity brand to all the right people at Nike World Headquarters.

Will Shelby sparked the flame and then Barb Frank carried the torch and ran with it. All of that love was right there on display at the opening of my 3rd location, and it was just an amazing feeling. Things were finally coming together. The dream was getting closer.

Brossard was our first location in a mall, and it was an A+ power centre.

Exclucity was now beside some of the biggest brands in North America and that solidified the brand even more.

With three locations opened and a fourth on the way, Exclucity was becoming a legit brand and no longer just a local shop. We were now a major player in the game.

With Brossard up and running, I turned my attention back to Laval. I finalized the lease and made plans to open on July 15, 2014.

. . .

Laval, The 4th Location

With all eyes on me, and knowing that Laval would be the last store I opened in Montreal before tackling the national market, I wanted to do something HUGE! I set out to have the biggest opening and the biggest restock EVER.

Yes, I wanted to make history not only with the restock and the party, but I also wanted a bigger and better experience for the customer.

The Brossard opening was amazing but the lineup wasn't organized properly. It was a bit all over the place because I had too much stuff going on. I was focused on fixing that.

I also had the pressure of trying to live up to Gentry as the host but I had a plan.

But before I tell you about that, let me finally tell you about "The Uniform Boys" and why I don't like them.

. . .

Unfortunately, as you get bigger you also draw more attention to yourself, which makes you a target. I was making a lot of noise in the Canadian sneaker world and I don't think "The Uniform Boys" liked that too much. Remember earlier when I told you that I had a beef with them. This is when it got worse and the line in the sand was drawn.

After I announced that the Laval opening was going to be our biggest ever and released my massive restock list, "The Uniform Boys" allegedly called up Nike to complain. They allegedly tried to stop my opening. I use the word "allegedly" to avoid a lawsuit but….

Apparently, they were pissed off at all the hype I was creating with my openings and they wanted it to stop. CAN YOU FUCKING BELIEVE IT? A billion-dollar company was rattled by something I was doing. They were upset because they were planning a new store opening of their own in October in Montreal and my restock and events were bigger than theirs.

They didn't like that so they allegedly complained to Nike, and tried to block me.

Since they couldn't stop me from opening, they tried to lessen the hype surrounding the opening and allegedly complained to Nike about us using the word "restock." Their claim was that since the product wasn't restocking at other retailers, we shouldn't be allowed to use the word, "restock." Now keep in mind that many other stores around the world had used the word for many years before this, but now all of a sudden it was a problem. It made no sense.

Regardless of the ridiculousness of their claim, the marketplace director at Nike called and asked me if I could take down the advertisements and redo them without using the word.

At first, I was pissed off but then I looked at it as an accomplishment. "The Uniform Boys" just made me look even better in Nike's eyes. For them to, allegedly, be calling and bitching about me meant that I was considered a threat. I used it as motivation and fuel to drive me to have an even bigger opening.

I took down all the advertisements and redid everything; it didn't stop my momentum one bit. It was just a waste of time; my opening was still going to be bigger and better than theirs.

After I dealt with that ridiculous issue, I resumed my planning of the opening.

. . .

The first thing I focused on was the client experience. The problem with the Brossard opening was that customers were staying at the cash register for too long trying to find out what sizes were left. At the beginning of the day, it wasn't such a problem but as sizes start to sell out, that's when it became an issue because there were hundreds of people waiting in line behind them.

To fix the problem and have the line move faster, I had the staff set up four iPads that were able to check our live inventory. On the day of the opening, we had four staff members on iPads; two outside and two inside working with customers and letting them know what we had left in stock, and what had been sold out.

Once you made your purchase, you went to the other side of the store to pick up your purchase and left through the other door. It was like a pipeline of flowing traffic and worked out perfectly.

We did three times as much business during the Laval opening than we did with the Brossard one.

. . .

Next issue to solve; who was going to be my host?

If Gentry Humphrey was one of five guys who helped create sneaker culture, then DJ Clark Kent "God's Favourite DJ" (That's his nickname, I swear) is one of the Top 5 sneakerheads in the world. How cool would it be to have him host the opening?

ABC's 'Nightline' did a special on Sneaker Culture and they asked DJ Clark Kent to be their special guest. That's how big he was. "In the world of Sneaker Heads, DJ Clark Kent is the President," said the late-night television news program.

DJ Clark Kent isn't only known for his sneakers, he also played a role in discovering and signing Biggie Smalls and Jay-Z.

He's a legend and it was an honour to have him host but it was also stressful because he almost didn't make it.

I booked Kent's flight to arrive in Montreal Friday night, as we were opening Saturday morning. Everything was set up just fine but then his manager called me Thursday night and told me that Jay-Z had called him to book Kent for a last-minute DJ gig at a concert Friday night. He wanted to know if it would be okay with me if Kent flew in Saturday morning, instead of Friday night as planned.

All I could think of was wtf would I do if Kent missed the Saturday morning flight out of NYC. It scared the shit out of me. I urged him to not take the gig with Jay-Z so that he could still come on the Friday night flight as planned. If something happened to his flight Saturday morning and he missed it, it would be the biggest embarrassment of my life, and I wouldn't be able to show my face around Montreal again, I told him.

Kent is such a good dude that he totally understood where I was coming from and flew in on Friday night. I took him out for an expensive steak dinner that night, but I'm sure it was nothing compared to a night with Jay-Z and Beyoncé. But on the other hand, he's had many nights with them and I'm sure he'll have plenty more.

. . .

That Laval opening was no doubt our biggest TO DATE. Some say it was the biggest restock in Canadian history. (But I don't want to brag).

The leasing company said it was the biggest store opening they had ever seen in their 60-year history. The line was massive, it wrapped around the mall and not in a single file either.

We opened our doors at 10am and the line didn't finish till 8pm that night. We had people from all over Montreal, Ottawa, Toronto, and even New York City. Someone told me they flew in from California to be at the opening.

We have a five-minute video of each of our store openings on our site. Just go to shop.exclucitylife.com and then go to the 'about us' section. They are all there; it's really cool to see it all go down.

While you're on the site, feel free to visit the other sections and buy something. (You see the marketing right there. I never stop working, NEVER !!! lol!)

. . .

Mission Accomplished

After that Laval opening, I'd go on to open my first store in Toronto on July 25, 2015 and continued opening more stores, officially becoming a national brand.

What I was able to do in Montreal as a sneaker boutique had never been done before. Quebec is labelled as one of the most difficult territories in all of Canada to break into, and they say if you can make it there then you could make it anywhere.

To date, Exclucity is the fastest growing regional account in Nike Canada's history, and for five years straight Exclucity was Nike's largest regional account in Canada.

. . .

How did sneakers save my life?

A lot of people encourage their kids to go into sports as a way out. While sports is great for kids because it keeps them out of trouble and builds teamwork skills, I'll be encouraging my kids to be owners and entrepreneurs. I'll push them just as hard into ownership, as soccer moms push their kids from the sidelines.

True financial freedom comes from **ownership**, and the most important part of the statement is **freedom**, and not financial. Fuck the financial part, the money will come and go, it's the freedom that will give you the life that you truly want. That's where true happiness resides, and that's what sneakers gave me.

Freedom.

. . .

The Next Five Years

After opening my first store in Toronto in 2015, the next five years of my life would be the most terrifying, stressful and depressing years of my entire life. Had it not been for the pandemic in 2020, I don't think I would have survived. I was spiraling out of control and it was happening FAST!!!

To be continued...

BOOK 2

HOW SNEAKERS RUINED MY LIFE

My Entrepreneurial Journey That Shifted My Mental State

EXCLUCITY 3 | 2015 Sidelined by Nike

EXCLUCITY 4 | 2016 Adidas & YEZZY

EXCLUCITY 5 | 2017 Tier Zero

EXCLUCITY 6 | 2018 Losing $2.23 Million

EXCLUCITY 7 | 2019 Days Away from Bankruptcy

-

TRENT 3 | 2015 Thinking about ME

TRENT 4 | 2016 The Mansion

TRENT 5 | 2017 Poly-am-o-rous

TRENT 6 | 2018 Bipolar

TRENT 7 | 2019 Spiraling Out of Control

BOOK 3

HOW QUARANTINE SAVED MY LIFE

Before I go, just one last story.

A few years after I opened the store in Brossard, the "The Uniform Boys" wanted to open a location in the same mall I was in. The leasing company called me in for a meeting to see if I would release my exclusivity clause and allow "The Uniform Boys" in, and I said no. They proposed a bunch of things and I just said no. Then I said, let me think about it and get back to you, and I said NO again.

After a few weeks, I called them and said OK, OK. OK, perhaps maybe if you………..hmmm actually, it's still a HELL NO!

Hope you enjoy the book… See you for Book 2 & 3

BYE!!!!!

Author: TRENT

Editor: Neil Armstrong

Photographer: NASKADEMINI

Art Director: Marcus Troy

Graphic Designer: AJ Saludo